THE COMPLETE

NINJA DUAL ZONE

Air Fryer

COOKBOOK FOR UK

Master the Art of Effortless Dual Zone Air Frying
with Mouthwatering Recipes for Beginners | UK
Measurements | Enhanced with Vibrant Pictures

Marty Mueller

TABLE OF
CONTENT

INTRODUCTION

Greetings, fellow cooking enthusiasts!

I am Marty Mueller, I am delighted to present to you my latest culinary endeavor, a cookbook dedicated to the remarkable Ninja Dual Zone Air Fryer. As a professional chef with years of experience in the kitchen, I have had the pleasure of exploring countless cooking techniques and appliances. However, the Ninja Dual Zone Air Fryer has truly captured my attention and sparked my creativity like no other.

Throughout my culinary journey, I have discovered that a well-designed air fryer can revolutionize the way we prepare our meals. The Ninja Dual Zone Air Fryer, with its cutting-edge features and exceptional performance, has inspired me to share my passion for this appliance with all of you. Hence, this cookbook is born.

Why have I chosen to dedicate an entire cookbook to the Ninja Dual Zone Air Fryer, you may ask? Well, let me tell you about the incredible possibilities this appliance offers. With its dual-zone cooking capability, you can simultaneously prepare a main course and a side dish, or even cook for two entirely different tastes or dietary needs. It's like having two air fryers in one! This versatility opens up a world of culinary opportunities, making meal preparation more efficient and exciting.

In this cookbook, you will find an enticing collection of over 100 recipes that showcase the versatility of the Ninja Dual Zone Air Fryer. From breakfast to dinner, from snacks to desserts, this cookbook has it all.

Start your day off right with a range of delicious breakfast recipes. Imagine waking up to the aroma of perfectly cooked bacon and eggs, crispy hash browns, or even fluffy pancakes—all prepared effortlessly in the air fryer. With the Ninja Dual Zone Air Fryer, breakfast has never been easier or more satisfying.

For main courses, the possibilities are endless. Explore an array of recipes featuring succulent meats, tender seafood, and vibrant vegetarian options. Imagine sinking your teeth into juicy air-fried burgers, savoring perfectly seasoned and crispy fried chicken, or relishing the flakiness of air-fried salmon fillets. Vegetarian options like crispy tofu nuggets or roasted vegetable medleys will also leave you satisfied and amazed by the flavours achieved using the Ninja Dual Zone Air Fryer.

As for sides and accompaniments, prepare to elevate your meals to new heights. Discover the pleasure of crispy sweet potato fries, perfectly roasted Brussels sprouts, or even air-fried mac and cheese bites. These recipes will not only complement your main dishes but also become household favorites.

Of course, we couldn't forget about desserts! Indulge your sweet tooth with guilt-free treats that come out of the air fryer perfectly caramelized, with a delightful crunch. Picture warm and gooey chocolate chip cookies, cinnamon-dusted churros, or even crispy apple turnovers—each bite will be a moment of pure bliss.

To enhance your cooking experience, this cookbook is beautifully illustrated with vibrant, full-colour pictures of the finished dishes. These visual representations will inspire and guide you, allowing you to see how each recipe should look, right down to the enticing golden crispiness and mouthwatering presentation.

So, whether you're looking to impress guests with a stunning dinner, surprise your family with a delectable breakfast, or simply treat yourself to a delightful snack, this cookbook has the perfect recipe for every occasion. With the Ninja Dual Zone Air Fryer and this cookbook in your hands, your culinary possibilities will expand, and your kitchen will become a hub of creativity and flavour.

Don't miss out on the chance to embark on this culinary adventure. Purchase your copy of the cookbook today and unlock a world of delicious possibilities with the Ninja Dual Zone Air Fryer.

Happy cooking and bon appétit!

Marty Mueller

CHAPTER 1

BREAKFAST RECIPES

Golden Avocado Tempura

SERVES: 4

PREP TIME: 5 minutes
COOK TIME: 12 minutes

60 g bread crumbs
½ tsp. salt
1 avocado, pitted, peeled and sliced
Liquid from 1 tin white beans

1. Mix the bread crumbs and salt in a shallow bowl until well-incorporated.
2. Dip the avocado slices in the bean liquid, then into the bread crumbs.
3. Install a crisper plate in Zone 1 drawer. Place avocado slices in the drawer, taking care not to overlap any slices, then insert drawer in unit.
4. Select Zone 1, select AIR FRY, set temperature to 180°C, and set time to 12 minutes. Press the START/PAUSE button to begin cooking.
5. With 6 minutes remaining, press START/PAUSE to pause the unit. Remove the drawer from unit and shake for 10 seconds. Reinsert drawer in unit and press START/PAUSE to resume cooking.
6. When cooking is complete, remove drawer from unit. Transfer avocado slices to a plate. Serve warm.

Cream Bread

SERVES: 8

PREP TIME: 20 minutes
COOK TIME: 50 minutes

240 ml milk
1 large egg
415 g bread flour
70 g plain flour
20 g milk powder
180 ml whipping cream
1 tsp. salt
50 g fine sugar
10 g dry yeast

1. Grease two 18 x 10 cm cake pans.
2. Mix together all the dry ingredients with the wet ingredients to form a dough.
3. Divide the dough into 4 equal-sized balls and roll each ball into a rectangle.
4. Roll each rectangle like a Swiss roll tightly and place 2 rolls into each prepared cake pan. Keep aside for about 1 hour.
5. Insert a crisper plate in both drawers. Place one cake pan in each drawer.
6. Select Zone 1, select BAKE, set temperature to 190°C, and set time to 50 minutes. Select MATCH COOK to match Zone 2 settings to Zone 1. Select START/PAUSE to begin cooking.
7. When cooking is complete, remove the bread rolls from pans.
8. Cut each roll into desired size slices and serve warm.

Banana Bread

MAKES 2 LOAVES

PREP TIME: 10 minutes
COOK TIME: 22 minutes

2 ripe bananas, mashed
200 g sugar
1 large egg
60 g unsalted butter, melted
140 g plain flour
5 g baking soda
1 tsp. salt

1. Coat the insides of 2 mini loaf pans with cooking spray.
2. In a large mixing bowl, mix the bananas and sugar.
3. In a separate large mixing bowl, combine the egg, butter, flour, baking soda, and salt and mix well.
4. Add the banana mixture to the egg and flour mixture. Mix well.
5. Divide the batter evenly among the prepared pans.
6. Insert a crisper plate in both drawers. Place 1 loaf pan in each drawer.
7. Select Zone 1, select BAKE, set temperature to 180°C, and set time to 22 minutes. Select MATCH COOK to match Zone 2 settings to Zone 1. Select START/PAUSE to begin cooking. Insert a toothpick into the centre of each loaf; if it comes out clean, they are done.
8. When the loaves are cooked through, remove the pans from the drawers. Turn out the loaves onto a wire rack to cool.
9. Serve warm.

Nutty Courgette Bread

SERVES 6

PREP TIME: 15 minutes
COOK TIME: 20 minutes

375 g plain flour
10 g baking powder
3 eggs
300 g courgette, grated
100 g walnuts, chopped

8 g ground cinnamon
1 tsp. salt
400 g white sugar
240 ml vegetable oil
15 ml vanilla extract

1. Grease two (18 x10 cm) loaf pans.
2. Mix together the flour, baking powder, cinnamon and salt in a bowl.
3. Whisk together eggs with sugar, vanilla extract and vegetable oil in a bowl until combined.
4. Stir in the flour mixture and fold in the courgette and walnuts.
5. Mix until combined and transfer the mixture into the prepared loaf pans.
6. Insert a crisper plate in both drawers. Place 1 loaf pan in each drawer.
7. Select Zone 1, select BAKE, set temperature to 160°C, and set time to 20 minutes. Select MATCH COOK to match Zone 2 settings to Zone 1. Select START/PAUSE to begin cooking.
8. When cooking is complete, remove from the Air fryer and place onto a wire rack to cool.
9. Cut the bread into desired size slices and serve.

Oat and Chia Porridge

SERVES: 4

PREP TIME: 10 minutes
COOK TIME: 8 minutes

30 g peanut butter
60 ml honey
15 g butter, melted
960 ml milk
200 g oats
160 g chia seeds

1. Put the peanut butter, honey, butter, and milk in a bowl and stir to mix. Add the oats and chia seeds and stir.
2. Transfer the mixture to two 18 x 13-cm baking dish.
3. Insert a crisper plate in both drawers. Place one baking dish in each drawer.
4. Select Zone 1, select BAKE, set temperature to 200°C, and set time to 8 minutes. Select MATCH COOK to match Zone 2 settings to Zone 1. Select START/PAUSE to begin cooking.
5. Give another stir before serving.

Cherry Tomato Frittata

SERVES: 2

PREP TIME: 10 minutes
COOK TIME: 12 minutes

½ of Italian sausage
4 cherry tomatoes, halved
3 eggs
15 g Parmesan cheese, shredded
1 g fresh parsley, chopped
15 ml olive oil
Salt and black pepper, to taste

1. Place the sausage and tomatoes in a 18x13 cm baking dish.
2. Install a crisper plate in Zone 1 drawer. Place baking dish in the drawer, then insert drawer in unit.
3. Select Zone 1, select BAKE, set temperature to 180°C, and set time to 12 minutes. Press the START/PAUSE button to begin cooking.
4. Whisk together eggs with Parmesan cheese, oil, parsley, salt and black pepper and beat until combined.
5. With 6 minutes remaining, press START/PAUSE to pause the unit. Remove the drawer from unit. Drizzle the cheese mixture over sausage and tomatoes. Reinsert drawers in unit and press START/PAUSE to resume cooking.
6. When cooking is complete, remove drawer from unit. Serve warm.

Kale and Potato Nuggets

SERVES: 4

PREP TIME: 10 minutes
COOK TIME: 18 minutes

5 ml extra virgin olive oil
1 clove garlic, minced
300 g kale, rinsed and chopped
400 g potatoes, boiled and mashed
30 ml milk
Salt and ground black pepper, to taste
Cooking spray

1. In a frying pan over medium heat, sauté the garlic in the olive oil, until it turns golden brown. Sauté with the kale for an additional 3 minutes and remove from the heat.
2. Mix the mashed potatoes, kale and garlic in a bowl. Pour in the milk and sprinkle with salt and pepper.
3. Shape the mixture into nuggets and spritz with cooking spray.
4. Install a crisper plate in Zone 1 drawer. Place nuggets in the drawer, then insert drawer in unit.
5. Select Zone 1, select AIR FRY, set temperature to 200°C, and set time to 15 minutes. Press the START/PAUSE button to begin cooking.
6. With 7 minutes remaining, press START/PAUSE to pause the unit. Remove the drawer from unit and flip the nuggets over. Reinsert drawer in unit and press START/PAUSE to resume cooking.
7. When cooking is complete, remove drawer from unit. Transfer nuggets to a plate. Serve warm.

Quick and Easy Blueberry Muffins

MAKES 8 MUFFINS

PREP TIME: 10 minutes
COOK TIME: 15 minutes

160 g flour
100 g sugar
10 g baking powder
¼ tsp. salt
80 ml rapeseed oil
1 egg
120 ml milk
100 g blueberries, fresh or frozen and thawed

1. In a medium bowl, stir together flour, sugar, baking powder, and salt.
2. In a separate bowl, combine oil, egg, and milk and mix well.
3. Add egg mixture to dry ingredients and stir just until moistened.
4. Gently stir in the blueberries.
5. Spoon batter evenly into parchment-paper-lined muffin cups.
6. Insert a crisper plate in both drawers. Place 4 muffin cups in each drawer.
7. Select Zone 1, select BAKA, set temperature to 160°C, and set time to 15 minutes. Select MATCH COOK to match Zone 2 settings to Zone 1. Select START/PAUSE to begin cooking, until tops spring back when touched lightly.
8. When cooking is complete, transfer muffin cups and serve warm.

Spinach Omelette

SERVES: 1

PREP TIME: 10 minutes
COOK TIME: 10 minutes

5 ml olive oil
3 eggs
Salt and ground black pepper, to taste
15 g ricotta cheese
30 g chopped spinach
3 g chopped parsley

1. Grease a 18 x13 cm baking dish with olive oil.
2. In a bowl, beat the eggs with a fork and sprinkle salt and pepper.
3. Add the ricotta, spinach, and parsley. Transfer the mixture into the baking dish.
4. Install a crisper plate in Zone 1 drawer. Place baking dish in the drawer, then insert drawer in unit.
5. Select Zone 1, select AIR FRY, set temperature to 165°C, and set time to 10 minutes. Press the START/PAUSE button to begin cooking, until the egg is set.
6. Serve warm.

Perfect Cheesy Eggs

SERVES: 2

PREP TIME: 10 minutes
COOK TIME: 12 minutes

10 g unsalted butter, softened
55 g ham, sliced thinly
4 large eggs, divided
25 g Parmesan cheese, grated finely
2 g fresh chives, minced
30 ml double cream
⅛ tsp. smoked paprika
Salt and black pepper, to taste

1. Grease a 13 cm pie pan with butter.
2. Whisk together 1 egg with cream, salt and black pepper in a bowl.
3. Place ham slices in the bottom of the pie pan and top with the egg mixture.
4. Crack the remaining eggs on top and season with smoked paprika, salt and black pepper. Top evenly with Parmesan cheese and chives.
5. Install a crisper plate in Zone 1 drawer. Place the pie pan in the drawer, then insert drawer in unit.
6. Select Zone 1, select BAKE, set temperature to 160°C, and set time to 12 minutes. Press the START/PAUSE button to begin cooking.
7. When cooking is complete, serve with toasted bread slices.

Mushroom and Squash Toast

SERVES: 4

PREP TIME: 10 minutes
COOK TIME: 15 minutes

15 ml olive oil
1 red bell pepper, cut into strips
2 spring onions, sliced
225 g sliced button or chestnut mushrooms
1 small yellow squash, sliced
30 g softened butter
4 slices bread
115 g soft goat cheese

1. Add the red pepper, spring onions, mushrooms, and squash in a bowl, and stir well.
2. Spread the butter on the slices of bread.
3. Insert a crisper plate in both drawer and brush with the olive oil. Place vegetables in the Zone 1 drawer, then insert drawer in unit. Place slices of bread in the Zone 2 drawer, butter-side up, then insert drawer in unit.
4. Select Zone 1, select AIR FRY, set temperature to 200°C, and set time to 15 minutes. Select Zone 2, select BAKE, set temperature to 180°C, and set time to 6 minutes. Select SYNC. Press the START/ PAUSE button to begin cooking.
5. When cooking is complete, transfer the bread slices to a plate. Top with goat cheese and vegetables. Serve warm.

Cornflakes Toast Sticks

SERVES: 4

PREP TIME: 10 minutes
COOK TIME: 8 minutes

2 eggs
120 ml milk
⅛ tsp. salt
½ tsp. pure vanilla extract
80 g crushed cornflakes
6 slices sandwich bread, each slice cut into 4 strips
Maple syrup, for dipping
Cooking spray

1. In a small bowl, beat together the eggs, milk, salt, and vanilla.
2. Put crushed cornflakes on a plate or in a shallow dish.
3. Dip bread strips in egg mixture, shake off excess, and roll in corn-flake crumbs.
4. Spray both sides of bread strips with cooking spray.
5. Insert a crisper plate in both drawers. Place half of the bread strips in a single layer in each drawer.
6. Select Zone 1, select AIR FRY, set temperature to 200°C, and set time to 8 minutes. Select MATCH COOK to match Zone 2 settings to Zone 1. Select START/PAUSE to begin cooking.
7. When the Zone 1 and 2 times reach 4 minutes, press START/PAUSE to pause the unit. Remove the drawers from unit and flip the bread strips over. Reinsert drawers in unit and press START/PAUSE to resume cooking.
8. When cooking is complete, transfer bread strips to a plate. Serve warm with maple syrup.

English Pumpkin Egg Bake

SERVES: 2

PREP TIME: 10 minutes
COOK TIME: 10 minutes

2 eggs
120 ml milk
250 g flour
30 ml cider vinegar
10 g baking powder
15 g sugar
225 g pumpkin purée
2 g cinnamon powder
5 g baking soda
15 ml olive oil

1. Crack the eggs into a bowl and beat with a whisk. Combine with the milk, flour, cider vinegar, baking powder, sugar, pumpkin purée, cinnamon powder, and baking soda, mixing well.
2. Grease a 18 x 13-cm baking dish with oil.
3. Install a crisper plate in Zone 1 drawer. Add the mixture in the baking dish and arrange in the drawer, then insert drawer in unit.
4. Select Zone 1, select BAKE, set temperature to 150°C, and set time to 10 minutes. Press the START/PAUSE button to begin cooking.
5. When cooking is complete, serve warm.

Lush Vegetable Omelette

SERVES: 2

PREP TIME: 10 minutes
COOK TIME: 13 minutes

10 ml rapeseed oil
4 eggs, whisked
45 ml plain milk
5 g melted butter
1 red bell pepper, seeded and chopped
1 green bell pepper, seeded and chopped
1 white onion, finely chopped
50 g baby spinach leaves, roughly chopped
50 g Halloumi cheese, shaved
Salt and freshly ground black pepper, to taste

1. Grease a 18 x 13-cm baking pan with rapeseed oil.
2. Put the remaining ingredients in the baking pan and stir well.
3. Install a crisper plate in Zone 1 drawer. Place the baking pan in the drawer, then insert drawer in unit.
4. Select Zone 1, select AIR FRY, set temperature to 180°C, and set time to 13 minutes. Press the START/PAUSE button to begin cooking.
5. When cooking is complete, serve warm.

CHAPTER 2
VEGETABLES RECIPES

Courgette Salad

SERVES: 4

PREP TIME: 15 minutes
COOK TIME: 18 minutes

450 g courgette, cut into rounds
500 g fresh spinach, chopped
30 g feta cheese, crumbled
30 ml olive oil
1 tsp. garlic powder
Salt and black pepper, as required
30 ml fresh lemon juice

1. Mix the courgette, oil, garlic powder, salt, and black pepper in a bowl and toss to coat well.
2. Install a crisper plate in Zone 1 drawer. Place courgette slices in the drawer, then insert drawer in unit.
3. Select Zone 1, select AIR FRY, set temperature to 200°C, and set time to 18 minutes. Press the START/PAUSE button to begin cooking.
4. With 9 minutes remaining, press START/PAUSE to pause the unit. Remove the drawer from unit and flip the courgette slices over. Reinsert drawer in unit and press START/PAUSE to resume cooking.
5. When cooking is complete, remove drawer from unit. Transfer courgette slices to a plate and keep aside to cool.
6. Add spinach, feta cheese, lemon juice, a little bit of salt and black pepper and mix well. Toss to coat well and serve immediately.

Tofu with Orange Sauce

SERVES: 4

PREP TIME: 20 minutes
COOK TIME: 16 minutes

450 g extra-firm tofu, pressed and cubed
120 ml water
16 g cornflour
2 spring onions (green part), chopped
15 ml tamari
80 ml fresh orange juice
15 ml honey
1 tsp. orange zest, grated
1 tsp. garlic, minced
1 tsp. fresh ginger, minced
¼ tsp. red pepper flakes, crushed

1. Mix the tofu, cornflour, and tamari in a bowl and toss to coat well.
2. Insert a crisper plate in both drawers. Place half of the tofu pieces in a single layer in each drawer.
3. Select Zone 1, select AIR FRY, set temperature to 200°C, and set time to 16 minutes. Select MATCH COOK to match Zone 2 settings to Zone 1. Select START/PAUSE to begin cooking.
4. When the Zone 1 and 2 times reach 8 minutes, press START/PAUSE to pause the unit. Remove the drawers from unit and tofu pieces over. Reinsert drawers in unit and press START/PAUSE to resume cooking.
5. When cooking is complete, transfer tofu pieces to a plate.
6. Put all the ingredients except spring onions in a small pan over medium-high heat and bring to a boil.
7. Pour this sauce over the tofu and garnish with spring onions to serve.

Perfectly Roasted Mushrooms

SERVES: 4

PREP TIME: 10 minutes
COOK TIME: 25 minutes

15 g butter, melted
900 g mushrooms, quartered
30 ml white vermouth
2 g herbs de Provence
½ tsp. garlic powder

1. Mix herbs de Provence, garlic powder and butter and mushrooms in a large bowl.
2. Insert a crisper plate in both drawers. Place half of the mushrooms in a single layer in each drawer.
3. Select Zone 1, select AIR FRY, set temperature to 200°C, and set time to 25 minutes. Select MATCH COOK to match Zone 2 settings to Zone 1. Select START/PAUSE to begin cooking.
4. When the Zone 1 and 2 times reach 5 minutes, press START/PAUSE to pause the unit. Remove the drawers from unit and stir the mushrooms with white vermouth. Reinsert drawers in unit and press START/PAUSE to resume cooking.
5. When cooking is complete, transfer the mushrooms to a plate. Serve warm.

Hasselback Potatoes

SERVES: 4

PREP TIME: 20 minutes
COOK TIME: 30 minutes

4 potatoes
16 g Parmesan cheese, shredded
3 g fresh chives, chopped
30 ml olive oil

1. Cut slits along each potato about 0.5 cm apart with a sharp knife, making sure slices should stay connected at the bottom.
2. Install a crisper plate in Zone 1 drawer. Coat the potatoes with olive oil and arrange in the drawer, then insert drawer in unit.
3. Select Zone 1, select AIR FRY, set temperature to 200°C, and set time to 30 minutes. Press the START/PAUSE button to begin cooking.
4. When cooking is complete, remove drawer from unit. Transfer potatoes to a plate. Top with chives and Parmesan cheese to serve.

Broccoli with Olives

SERVES: 4

PREP TIME: 15 minutes
COOK TIME: 19 minutes

900 g broccoli, stemmed and cut into 2.5 cm florets
50 g Kalamata olives, halved and pitted
30 g Parmesan cheese, grated
30 ml olive oil
Salt and ground black pepper, as required
2 tsps. fresh lemon zest, grated

1. Boil the broccoli in a pot for about 4 minutes and drain well.
2. Mix broccoli, oil, salt, and black pepper in a bowl and toss to coat well.
3. Install a crisper plate in Zone 1 drawer. Place broccoli in the drawer, then insert drawer in unit.
4. Select Zone 1, select AIR FRY, set temperature to 200°C, and set time to 15 minutes. Press the START/PAUSE button to begin cooking.
5. With 8 minutes remaining, press START/PAUSE to pause the unit. Remove the drawer from unit and shake for 10 seconds. Reinsert drawer in unit and press START/PAUSE to resume cooking.
6. When cooking is complete, remove drawer from unit. Transfer broccoli to a plate. Stir in the olives, lemon zest and cheese and dish out to serve.

Chewy Glazed Parsnips

SERVES: 6

PREP TIME: 10 minutes
COOK TIME: 35 minutes

900 g parsnips, peeled and cut into 2.5-cm chunks
15 g butter, melted
30 ml maple syrup
1 tbsp. dried parsley flakes, crushed
¼ tsp. red pepper flakes, crushed

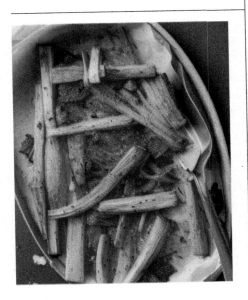

1. Mix parsnips and butter in a bowl and toss to coat well.
2. Insert a crisper plate in both drawers. Place half of the parsnips in each drawer.
3. Select Zone 1, select AIR FRY, set temperature to 200°C, and set time to 35 minutes. Select MATCH COOK to match Zone 2 settings to Zone 1. Select START/PAUSE to begin cooking.
4. When the Zone 1 and 2 times reach 15 minutes, press START/PAUSE to pause the unit. Remove the drawers from unit and shake for 10 seconds. Reinsert drawers in unit and press START/PAUSE to resume cooking.
5. Meanwhile, mix remaining ingredients in a large bowl.
6. When the Zone 1 and 2 times reach 5 minutes, press START/PAUSE to pause the unit. Remove the drawers from unit and spread the mixture over parsnips. Reinsert drawers in unit and press START/PAUSE to resume cooking.
7. When cooking is complete, transfer the parsnips to a plate. Serve warm.

Sweet and Sour Brussels Sprouts

SERVES: 2

PREP TIME: 10 minutes
COOK TIME: 16 minutes

300 g Brussels sprouts, trimmed and halved lengthwise
15 ml balsamic vinegar
15 ml maple syrup
Salt, as required

1. Mix all the ingredients in a bowl and toss to coat well.
2. Install a crisper plate in Zone 1 drawer. Place Brussels sprouts in the drawer, then insert drawer in unit.
3. Select Zone 1, select AIR FRY, set temperature to 200°C, and set time to 16 minutes. Press the START/PAUSE button to begin cooking.
4. With 8 minutes remaining, press START/PAUSE to pause the unit. Remove the drawer from unit and flip the Brussels sprouts over. Reinsert drawer in unit and press START/PAUSE to resume cooking.
5. When cooking is complete, remove drawer from unit. Transfer Brussels sprouts to a plate. Serve warm.

Easy Glazed Carrots

SERVES: 4

PREP TIME: 10 minutes
COOK TIME: 16 minutes

400 g carrots, peeled and cut into large chunks
15 ml olive oil
15 ml honey
Salt and black pepper, to taste

1. Mix all the ingredients in a bowl and toss to coat well.
2. Install a crisper plate in Zone 1 drawer. Place carrots in the drawer, then insert drawer in unit.
3. Select Zone 1, select AIR FRY, set temperature to 200°C, and set time to 16 minutes. Press the START/PAUSE button to begin cooking.
4. With 8 minutes remaining, press START/PAUSE to pause the unit. Remove the drawer from unit and flip the carrots over. Reinsert drawer in unit and press START/PAUSE to resume cooking.
5. When cooking is complete, remove drawer from unit. Transfer carrots to a plate. Serve warm.

Bell Peppers Cups

SERVES: 4

PREP TIME: 10 minutes
COOK TIME: 15 minutes

8 mini red bell peppers, tops and seeds removed
1 g fresh parsley, chopped
90 g feta cheese, crumbled
7 ml olive oil
Freshly ground black pepper, to taste

1. Mix feta cheese, parsley, olive oil and black pepper in a bowl.
2. Stuff the bell peppers with feta cheese mixture.
3. Insert a crisper plate in both drawers. Place 4 bell peppers in a single layer in each drawer.
4. Select Zone 1, select AIR FRY, set temperature to 200°C, and set time to 15 minutes. Select MATCH COOK to match Zone 2 settings to Zone 1. Select START/PAUSE to begin cooking.
5. When cooking is complete, transfer bell peppers to a plate. Serve warm.

Rice and Beans Stuffed Bell Peppers

SERVES: 5

PREP TIME: 15 minutes
COOK TIME: 16 minutes

425 g tinned diced tomatoes with juice
425 g tinned red kidney beans, rinsed and drained
150 g cooked rice
5 large bell peppers, tops removed and seeded
60 g mozzarella cheese, shredded
1½ tsps. Italian seasoning

1. Mix rice, tomatoes with juice, beans, and Italian seasoning in a bowl.
2. Halve the bell peppers and stuff the rice mixture in each bell pepper half.
3. Insert a crisper plate in both drawers. Place half of the stuffed bell peppers in a single layer in each drawer.
4. Select Zone 1, select BAKE, set temperature to 200°C, and set time to 16 minutes. Select MATCH COOK to match Zone 2 settings to Zone 1. Select START/PAUSE to begin cooking.
5. When the Zone 1 and 2 times reach 8 minutes, press START/PAUSE to pause the unit. Remove the drawers from unit and top the bell peppers with mozzarella cheese. Reinsert drawers in unit and press START/PAUSE to resume cooking.
6. When cooking is complete, transfer bell peppers to a plate. Serve warm.

Family Favourite Potatoes

SERVES: 4

PREP TIME: 10 minutes
COOK TIME: 22 minutes

800 g waxy potatoes, cubed and boiled
120 ml Greek plain yoghurt
30 ml olive oil, divided
1 tbsp. paprika, divided
Salt and black pepper, to taste

1. Mix 15 ml olive oil, ⅓ tbsp. of paprika, black pepper and potatoes in a bowl and toss to coat well.
2. Install a crisper plate in Zone 1 drawer. Place potatoes in the drawer, then insert drawer in unit.
3. Select Zone 1, select AIR FRY, set temperature to 200°C, and set time to 22 minutes. Press the START/PAUSE button to begin cooking.
4. With 11 minutes remaining, press START/PAUSE to pause the unit. Remove the drawer from unit and shake for 10 seconds. Reinsert drawer in unit and press START/PAUSE to resume cooking.
5. When cooking is complete, remove drawer from unit. Transfer potatoes to a plate. Mix yoghurt, remaining oil, salt and black pepper in a bowl and serve with potatoes.

Cauliflower Salad

SERVES: 4

PREP TIME: 20 minutes
COOK TIME: 20 minutes

40 g golden sultanas
240 g boiling water
1 head cauliflower, cut into small florets
40 g pecans, toasted and chopped
60 ml olive oil
1 tbsp. curry powder
Salt, to taste
For the Dressing:
240 ml mayonnaise
30 g coconut sugar
15 ml fresh lemon juice

1. Mix the cauliflower, pecans, curry powder, salt, and olive oil in a bowl and toss to coat well.
2. Install a crisper plate in Zone 1 drawer. Place cauliflower florets in the drawer, then insert drawer in unit.
3. Select Zone 1, select ROAST, set temperature to 200°C, and set time to 20 minutes. Press the START/PAUSE button to begin cooking.
4. Meanwhile, add the sultanas in boiling water in a bowl for about 20 minutes.
5. With 10 minutes remaining, press START/PAUSE to pause the unit. Remove the drawer from unit and flip the cauliflower florets over. Reinsert drawer in unit and press START/PAUSE to resume cooking.
6. When cooking is complete, remove drawer from unit. Transfer cauliflower florets to a plate. Drain the sultanas well and mix with the cauliflower florets.
7. Mix all the ingredients for dressing in a bowl and pour over the salad.
8. Toss to coat well and serve immediately.

Stuffed Pumpkin

SERVES: 4

PREP TIME: 20 minutes
COOK TIME: 35 minutes

2 tomatoes, chopped
1 bell pepper, chopped
1 beetroot, chopped
70 g green beans, shelled
½ of butternut pumpkin, seeded
2 garlic cloves, minced
2 tsps. mixed dried herbs
Salt and black pepper, to taste

1. Mix all the ingredients in a bowl except pumpkin and toss to coat well.
2. Install a crisper plate in Zone 1 drawer. Stuff the vegetable mixture into the pumpkin and place in the drawer, then insert drawer in unit.
3. Select Zone 1, select ROAST, set temperature to 180°C, and set time to 35 minutes. Press the START/PAUSE button to begin cooking.
4. When cooking is complete, remove drawer from unit. Transfer pumpkin to a plate and keep aside to slightly cool. Serve warm.

Breadcrumbs Stuffed Mushrooms

SERVES: 4

PREP TIME: 15 minutes
COOK TIME: 15 minutes

1½ spelt bread slices
2 g flat-leaf parsley, finely chopped
16 small button mushrooms, stemmed and gills removed
22 ml olive oil
1 garlic clove, crushed
Salt and black pepper, to taste

1. Put the bread slices in a food processor and pulse until fine crumbs form.
2. Transfer the crumbs into a bowl and stir in the olive oil, garlic, parsley, salt, and black pepper.
3. Stuff the breadcrumbs mixture in each mushroom cap.
4. Insert a crisper plate in both drawers. Place half of mushroom caps in a single layer in each drawer.
5. Select Zone 1, select AIR FRY, set temperature to 200°C, and set time to 15 minutes. Select MATCH COOK to match Zone 2 settings to Zone 1. Select START/PAUSE to begin cooking.
6. When cooking is complete, transfer mushroom caps to a plate. Serve warm.

CHAPTER 3
FISH AND SEAFOOD RECIPES

Simple Salmon Patty Bites

SERVES: 4

PREP TIME: 15 minutes
COOK TIME: 15 minutes

4 (140 g) tins pink salmon, skinless, boneless in water, drained
2 eggs, beaten
100 g whole-wheat panko bread crumbs
60 g finely minced red bell pepper
2 tbsps. parsley flakes
2 tsps. Old Bay seasoning
Cooking spray

1. In a medium bowl, mix the salmon, eggs, panko bread crumbs, red bell pepper, parsley flakes, and Old Bay seasoning.
2. Using a small cookie scoop, form the mixture into 20 balls.
3. Insert a crisper plate in both drawers. Place half of salmon bites in a single layer in each drawer. Spray lightly with cooking spray.
4. Select Zone 1, select AIR FRY, set temperature to 200°C, and set time to 15 minutes. Select MATCH COOK to match Zone 2 settings to Zone 1. Select START/PAUSE to begin cooking.
5. When the Zone 1 and 2 times reach 8 minutes, press START/PAUSE to pause the unit. Remove the drawers from unit and flip the salmon bites over. Lightly spray with the cooking spray. Reinsert drawers in unit and press START/PAUSE to resume cooking.
6. When cooking is complete, transfer salmon bites to a plate. Serve warm.

Sesame Seeds Coated Haddock

SERVES: 4

PREP TIME: 15 minutes
COOK TIME: 18 minutes

32 g plain flour
2 eggs
50 g sesame seeds, toasted
50 g breadcrumbs

4 (170 g) frozen haddock fillets
⅛ tsp. dried rosemary, crushed
Salt and ground black pepper, as required
45 ml olive oil

1. Place the flour in a shallow bowl and whisk the eggs in a second bowl.
2. Mix sesame seeds, breadcrumbs, rosemary, salt, black pepper and olive oil in a third bowl until a crumbly mixture is formed.
3. Coat each fillet with flour, dip into whisked eggs and finally, dredge into the breadcrumb mixture
4. Insert a crisper plate in both drawers. Place 2 haddock fillets in a single layer in each drawer.
5. Select Zone 1, select AIR FRY, set temperature to 200°C, and set time to 18 minutes. Select MATCH COOK to match Zone 2 settings to Zone 1. Select START/PAUSE to begin cooking.
6. When the Zone 1 and 2 times reach 8 minutes, press START/PAUSE to pause the unit. Remove the drawers from unit and flip the haddock fillets over. Reinsert drawers in unit and press START/PAUSE to resume cooking.
7. When cooking is complete, transfer haddock fillets to a plate. Serve warm.

Crispy Halibut Strips

SERVES: 2

PREP TIME: 20 minutes
COOK TIME: 15 minutes

2 eggs
15 ml water
170 g plain panko breadcrumbs
340 g skinless halibut fillets, cut into 2.5 cm strips
4 tbsps. taco seasoning mix

1. Put the taco seasoning mix in a shallow bowl and whisk together eggs and water in a second bowl.
2. Place the breadcrumbs in a third bowl.
3. Dredge the halibut with taco seasoning mix, then dip into the egg mixture and finally, coat evenly with the breadcrumbs.
4. Insert a crisper plate in both drawers. Place half of halibut strips in a single layer in each drawer.
5. Select Zone 1, select AIR FRY, set temperature to 200°C, and set time to 15 minutes. Select MATCH COOK to match Zone 2 settings to Zone 1. Select START/PAUSE to begin cooking.
6. When the Zone 1 and 2 times reach 7 minutes, press START/PAUSE to pause the unit. Remove the drawers from unit and flip the halibut strips over. Reinsert drawers in unit and press START/PAUSE to resume cooking.
7. When cooking is complete, transfer halibut strips to a plate. Serve warm.

(Note: Taco seasoning mix - Mix chilli powder, garlic powder, onion powder, red pepper flakes, oregano, paprika, cumin, salt and pepper in a small bowl. Store in an airtight container.)

Cajun Spiced Salmon

SERVES: 2

PREP TIME: 10 minutes
COOK TIME: 12 minutes

2 (200 g) (2-cm thick) salmon fillets
1 tbsp. Cajun seasoning
2 g coconut sugar
15 ml fresh lemon juice

1. Season the salmon evenly with Cajun seasoning and coconut sugar.
2. Install a crisper plate in Zone 1 drawer. Place salmon fillets in the drawer, skin-side up, then insert drawer in unit.
3. Select Zone 1, select AIR FRY, set temperature to 200°C, and set time to 12 minutes. Press the START/PAUSE button to begin cooking.
4. When cooking is complete, remove drawer from unit. Transfer salmon fillets to a plate. Drizzle with the lemon juice and serve hot.

Cod with Asparagus

SERVES: 2

PREP TIME: 15 minutes
COOK TIME: 20 minutes

2 (170 g) boneless cod fillets
6 g fresh parsley, roughly chopped
6 g fresh dill, roughly chopped
1 bunch asparagus
1 tsp. dried basil
22 ml fresh lemon juice
15 ml olive oil
Salt and black pepper, to taste

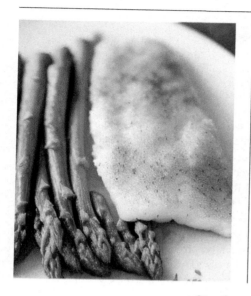

1. Mix lemon juice, oil, basil, salt, and black pepper in a small bowl.
2. Combine the cod and ¾ of the oil mixture in another bowl.
3. Coat asparagus with remaining oil mixture.
4. Insert a crisper plate in both drawers. Place cod in the Zone 1 drawer, then insert drawer in unit. Place asparagus in the Zone 2 drawer, then insert drawer in unit.
5. Select Zone 1, select AIR FRY, set temperature to 200°C, and set time to 15 minutes. Select Zone 2, select ROAST, set temperature to 200°C, and set time to 20 minutes. Select SYNC. Press the START/PAUSE button to begin cooking.
6. When the Zone 1 and 2 times reach 8 minutes, press START/PAUSE to pause the unit. Remove the drawers from unit and shake for 10 seconds. Reinsert drawers in unit and press START/PAUSE to resume cooking.
7. When cooking is complete, serve cod immediately with asparagus.

Salmon with Dill Sauce

SERVES: 2

PREP TIME: 15 minutes
COOK TIME: 10 minutes

2 (170 g) salmon fillets
120 ml Greek yoghurt
6 g fresh dill, chopped and divided
10 ml olive oil
Salt, to taste
60 g sour cream

1. Coat salmon with olive oil and season with a pinch of salt.
2. Install a crisper plate in Zone 1 drawer. Place salmon fillets in the drawer, then insert drawer in unit.
3. Select Zone 1, select ROAST, set temperature to 200°C, and set time to 10 minutes. Press the START/PAUSE button to begin cooking.
4. Meanwhile, mix remaining ingredients in a bowl to make dill sauce.
5. With 5 minutes remaining, press START/PAUSE to pause the unit. Remove the drawer from unit and flip the salmon fillets over. Reinsert drawer in unit and press START/PAUSE to resume cooking.
6. When cooking is complete, remove drawer from unit. Transfer salmon fillets to a plate. Serve the salmon with dill sauce.

Breaded Prawns with Lemon

SERVES: 3

PREP TIME: 15 minutes
COOK TIME: 10 minutes

60 g plain flour
2 egg whites
100 g breadcrumbs
450 g large prawns, peeled and deveined
Salt and ground black pepper, as required
¼ tsp. lemon zest
¼ tsp. cayenne pepper
¼ tsp. red pepper flakes, crushed
30 ml olive oil

1. Mix flour, salt, and black pepper in a shallow bowl.
2. Whisk the egg whites in a second bowl and mix the breadcrumbs, lime zest and spices in a third bowl.
3. Coat each prawn with the flour, dip into egg whites and finally, dredge in the breadcrumbs. Drizzle the prawns evenly with olive oil.
4. Insert a crisper plate in both drawers. Place half of the coated prawns in a single layer in each drawer.
5. Select Zone 1, select AIR FRY, set temperature to 200°C, and set time to 10 minutes. Select MATCH COOK to match Zone 2 settings to Zone 1. Select START/PAUSE to begin cooking.
6. When the Zone 1 and 2 times reach 5 minutes, press START/PAUSE to pause the unit. Remove the drawers from unit and flip the prawns over. Reinsert drawers in unit and press START/PAUSE to resume cooking.
7. When cooking is complete, transfer prawns to a plate. Serve hot.

Tuna Patty Sliders

SERVES: 4

PREP TIME: 15 minutes
COOK TIME: 15 minutes

3 (140 g) tins tuna, packed in water
70 g whole-wheat panko bread crumbs
40 g shredded Parmesan cheese
15 ml sriracha
¾ tsp. black pepper
10 whole-wheat slider buns
Cooking spray

1. In a medium bowl combine the tuna, bread crumbs, Parmesan cheese, sriracha, and black pepper and stir to combine.
2. Form the mixture into 10 patties.
3. Insert a crisper plate in both drawers. Place 5 patties in a single layer in each drawer. Spray the patties lightly with cooking spray.
4. Select Zone 1, select AIR FRY, set temperature to 200°C, and set time to 15 minutes. Select MATCH COOK to match Zone 2 settings to Zone 1. Select START/PAUSE to begin cooking.
5. When the Zone 1 and 2 times reach 8 minutes, press START/PAUSE to pause the unit. Remove the drawers from unit and flip the patties over. Lightly spray with the cooking spray. Reinsert drawers in unit and press START/PAUSE to resume cooking.
6. When cooking is complete, transfer patties to a plate. Serve the patties on buns.

Coconut Crusted Prawn and Tortilla Crisps

SERVES: 3

PREP TIME: 15 minutes
COOK TIME: 13 minutes

225 ml coconut milk
50 g sweetened coconut, shredded
50 g panko breadcrumbs
450 g large prawns, peeled and deveined
Salt and black pepper, to taste
3 corn tortillas
15 ml olive oil

1. Place the coconut milk in a shallow bowl.
2. Mix coconut, breadcrumbs, salt, and black pepper in another bowl.
3. Dip each prawn into coconut milk and finally, dredge in the coconut mixture.
4. Slice the corn tortillas into triangles. Coat with a light brushing of olive oil.
5. Insert a crisper plate in both drawers. Place prawns in the Zone 1 drawer, then insert drawer in unit. Place tortilla pieces in the Zone 2 drawer, then insert drawer in unit.
6. Select Zone 1, select AIR FRY, set temperature to 200°C, and set time to 13 minutes. Select Zone 2, select AIR FRY, set temperature to 200°C, and set time to 6 minutes. Select SYNC. Press the START/PAUSE button to begin cooking.
7. When cooking is complete, serve prawns with tortilla crisps.

Paprika Prawns and Brussels Sprouts

SERVES: 2

PREP TIME: 10 minutes
COOK TIME: 20 minutes

450 g tiger prawns
45 ml olive oil, divided
½ tsp. smoked paprika
450 g Brussels sprouts, trimmed and halved
30 g whole wheat breadcrumbs
30 g Parmesan cheese, shredded
15 ml balsamic vinegar
Salt and black pepper, to taste

1. Mix prawns, 30 ml olive oil, paprika and salt to taste in a large bowl until well combined.
2. Mix Brussels sprouts, vinegar, the remaining 15 ml oil, salt, and black pepper in another bowl and toss to coat well.
3. Insert a crisper plate in both drawers. Place prawns in the Zone 1 drawer, then insert drawer in unit. Place Brussels sprouts in the Zone 2 drawer, then insert drawer in unit.
4. Select Zone 1, select AIR FRY, set temperature to 200°C, and set time to 12 minutes. Select Zone 2, select ROAST, set temperature to 200°C, and set time to 20 minutes. Select SYNC. Press the START/PAUSE button to begin cooking.
5. When the Zone 1 and 2 times reach 8 minutes, press START/PAUSE to pause the unit. Remove the drawers from unit and shake for 10 seconds. Then sprinkle with breadcrumbs and cheese on Zone 2 drawer. Reinsert drawers in unit and press START/PAUSE to resume cooking.
6. When cooking is complete, serve prawns with Brussels sprouts.

Air Fried Spring Rolls

SERVES: 4

PREP TIME: 10 minutes
COOK TIME: 18 minutes

2 tsps. minced garlic
240 g finely sliced cabbage
110 g matchstick cut carrots
2 (110 g) tins tiny prawns, drained
20 ml soy sauce
Salt and freshly ground black pepper, to taste
16 square spring roll wrappers
Cooking spray

1. Spray a medium sauté pan with cooking spray.
2. Add the garlic to the sauté pan and cook over medium heat until fragrant, 30 to 45 seconds. Add the cabbage and carrots and sauté until the vegetables are slightly tender, about 5 minutes.
3. Add the prawns and soy sauce and season with salt and pepper, then stir to combine. Sauté until the moisture has evaporated, 2 more minutes. Set aside to cool.
4. Place a spring roll wrapper on a work surface so it looks like a diamond. Place 1 tbsp. of the prawn mixture on the lower end of the wrapper.
5. Roll the wrapper away from you halfway, then fold in the right and left sides, like an envelope. Continue to roll to the very end, using a little water to seal the edge. Repeat with the remaining wrappers and filling.
6. Insert a crisper plate in both drawers. Place half of spring rolls in a single layer in each drawer. Lightly spray with cooking spray.
7. Select Zone 1, select AIR FRY, set temperature to 190°C, and set time to 10 minutes. Select MATCH COOK to match Zone 2 settings to Zone 1. Select START/PAUSE to begin cooking.
8. When cooking is complete, transfer spring rolls to a plate. Let cool for 5 minutes before serving.

Prawn Magic

SERVES: 3

PREP TIME: 20 minutes
COOK TIME: 10 minutes

680 g prawns, peeled and deveined
Lemongrass stalks
4 garlic cloves, minced
1 red chilli pepper, seeded and chopped
30 ml olive oil
½ tsp. smoked paprika

1. Mix all the ingredients in a large bowl and refrigerate to marinate for about 2 hours.
2. Thread the prawns onto lemongrass stalks.
3. Insert a crisper plate in both drawers. Place half of prawns in a single layer in each drawer.
4. Select Zone 1, select ROAST, set temperature to 200°C, and set time to 10 minutes. Select MATCH COOK to match Zone 2 settings to Zone 1. Select START/PAUSE to begin cooking.
5. When the Zone 1 and 2 times reach 5 minutes, press START/PAUSE to pause the unit. Remove the drawers from unit and flip the prawns over. Reinsert drawers in unit and press START/PAUSE to resume cooking.
6. When cooking is complete, transfer prawns to a plate. Serve warm.

Cod and Veggies

SERVES: 4

PREP TIME: 20 minutes
COOK TIME: 25 minutes

30 g butter, melted
70 g red bell peppers, seeded and thinly sliced
70 g carrots, peeled and julienned
70 g fennel bulbs, julienned
2 (140 g) frozen cod fillets, thawed
15 ml fresh lemon juice
½ tsp. dried tarragon
Salt and ground black pepper, as required
15 ml olive oil

1. Mix butter, lemon juice, tarragon, salt, and black pepper in a large bowl.
2. Add the carrot, bell pepper and fennel bulb and generously coat with the butter mixture.
3. Coat the cod fillets with olive oil and season with salt and black pepper. Top with any remaining sauce from the bowl.
4. Insert a crisper plate in both drawers. Place cod fillets in the Zone 1 drawer, then insert drawer in unit. Place vegetables in the Zone 2 drawer, then insert drawer in unit.
5. Select Zone 1, select AIR FRY, set temperature to 200°C, and set time to 15 minutes. Select Zone 2, select AIR FRY, set temperature to 200°C, and set time to 25 minutes. Select SYNC. Press the START/PAUSE button to begin cooking.
6. When zones have finished cooking, check cod fillets for doneness. Transfer cod fillets to a plate and serve with vegetables.

Zesty Mahi Mahi

SERVES: 3

PREP TIME: 10 minutes
COOK TIME: 16 minutes

680 g Mahi Mahi fillets
1 lemon, cut into slices
3 g fresh dill, chopped
½ tsp. red chilli powder
Salt and ground black pepper, as required

1. Season the Mahi Mahi fillets evenly with chilli powder, salt, and black pepper.
2. Insert a crisper plate in both drawers. Place Mahi Mahi fillets in a single layer in each drawer. Top with the lemon slices.
3. Select Zone 1, select ROAST, set temperature to 200°C, and set time to 16 minutes. Select MATCH COOK to match Zone 2 settings to Zone 1. Select START/PAUSE to begin cooking.
4. When the Zone 1 and 2 times reach 8 minutes, press START/PAUSE to pause the unit. Remove the drawers from unit and flip the Mahi Mahi fillets over. Reinsert drawers in unit and press START/PAUSE to resume cooking.
5. When cooking is complete, transfer lemon slices to a plate. Place the lemon slices over the salmon. Garnish with fresh dill and serve warm.

CHAPTER 4
PORK RECIPES

Cheesy Sausage Balls

SERVES: 6

PREP TIME: 5 minutes
COOK TIME: 17 minutes

340 g pork sausage
170 g shredded Cheddar cheese
12 Cheddar cubes

1. Mix the shredded cheese and sausage.
2. Divide the mixture into 12 equal parts to be stuffed.
3. Add a cube of cheese to the centre of the sausage and roll into balls.
4. Insert a crisper plate in both drawers. Place half of balls in a single layer in each drawer.
5. Select Zone 1, select AIR FRY, set temperature to 200°C, and set time to 17 minutes. Select MATCH COOK to match Zone 2 settings to Zone 1. Select START/PAUSE to begin cooking.
6. When the Zone 1 and 2 times reach 8 minutes, press START/PAUSE to pause the unit. Remove the drawers from unit and flip the balls over. Reinsert drawers in unit and press START/PAUSE to resume cooking.
7. When cooking is complete, transfer balls to a plate. Serve warm.

Citrus Pork Loin Roast

SERVES: 8

PREP TIME: 10 minutes
COOK TIME: 40 minutes

15 ml lime juice
20 g orange marmalade
1 tsp. coarse brown mustard
1 tsp. curry powder
1 tsp. dried lemongrass
900 g boneless pork loin roast
Salt and ground black pepper, to taste
Cooking spray

1. Mix the lime juice, marmalade, mustard, curry powder, and lemongrass.
2. Rub mixture all over the surface of the pork loin. Season with salt and pepper.
3. Install a crisper plate in Zone 1 drawer. Place pork roast diagonally in the drawer and spray with cooking spray. then insert drawer in unit.
4. Select Zone 1, select ROAST, set temperature to 190°C, and set time to 40 minutes. Press the START/PAUSE button to begin cooking.
5. When cooking is complete, remove drawer from unit. Wrap roast in foil and let rest for 10 minutes before slicing.

Pork Spare Ribs

SERVES: 6

PREP TIME: 15 minutes
COOK TIME: 22 minutes

12 (2.5-cm) pork spare ribs
60 g cornflour
5-6 garlic cloves, minced
120 ml rice vinegar
30 ml soy sauce
30 ml olive oil
Salt and black pepper, to taste

1. Mix the garlic, vinegar, soy sauce, salt, and black pepper in a large bowl.
2. Coat the ribs generously with this mixture and refrigerate to marinate overnight.
3. Place the cornflour in a shallow bowl and dredge the ribs in it. Drizzle with olive oil.
4. Insert a crisper plate in both drawers. Place half of ribs in a single layer in each drawer.
5. Select Zone 1, select AIR FRY, set temperature to 190°C, and set time to 22 minutes. Select MATCH COOK to match Zone 2 settings to Zone 1. Select START/PAUSE to begin cooking.
6. When the Zone 1 and 2 times reach 10 minutes, press START/PAUSE to pause the unit. Remove the drawers from unit and flip the ribs over. Reinsert drawers in unit and press START/PAUSE to resume cooking.
7. When cooking is complete, transfer ribs to a plate. Serve warm.

Chinese Pork Meatballs with Brussels Sprouts

SERVES: 3

PREP TIME: 15 minutes
COOK TIME: 22 minutes

For The Meatballs:
1 egg, beaten
170 g minced pork
30 g cornflour
5 ml oyster sauce
7 ml light soy sauce
2 ml sesame oil
¼ tsp. five spice powder

7 ml olive oil
¼ tsp. honey
For the Brussels Sprouts:
300 g Brussels sprouts, trimmed and halved lengthwise
15 ml balsamic vinegar
15 ml maple syrup
Salt, as required

1. Mix all the ingredients for Brussels Sprouts in a bowl and toss to coat well.
2. Mix all the ingredients for the meatballs in a bowl except cornflour and oil until well combined.
3. Shape the mixture into equal-sized balls and place the cornflour in a shallow dish.
4. Roll the meatballs evenly into cornflour mixture.
5. Insert a crisper plate in both drawers. Place Brussels Sprouts in the Zone 1 drawer, then insert drawer in unit. Place meatballs in the Zone 2 drawer, then insert drawer in unit.
6. Select Zone 1, select ROAST, set temperature to 200°C, and set time to 22 minutes. Select Zone 2, select AIR FRY, set temperature to 190°C, and set time to 16 minutes. Select SYNC. Press the START/PAUSE button to begin cooking.
7. When the Zone 1 and Zone 2 times reach 8 minutes, press START/PAUSE and remove drawers from unit. In Zone 1, shake the Brussels Sprouts for 10 seconds. In Zone 2, flip the meatballs over. Reinsert drawers in unit and press START/PAUSE to resume cooking.
8. When cooking is complete, serve meatballs with Brussels Sprouts.

Pepper Pork Chops

SERVES: 2

PREP TIME: 15 minutes
COOK TIME: 16 minutes

2 pork chops
1 egg white
90 g xanthum gum
½ tsp. sea salt
¼ tsp. freshly ground black pepper
1 oil mister

1. Whisk egg white with salt and black pepper in a bowl and dip the pork chops in it.
2. Cover the bowl and marinate for about 20 minutes.
3. Pour the xanthum gum over both sides of the chops and spray with oil mister.
4. Install a crisper plate in Zone 1 drawer. Place chops in the drawer, then insert drawer in unit.
5. Select Zone 1, select ROAST, set temperature to 190°C, and set time to 16 minutes. Press the START/PAUSE button to begin cooking.
6. With 8 minutes remaining, press START/PAUSE to pause the unit. Remove the drawer from unit and flip the chops over. Reinsert drawer in unit and press START/PAUSE to resume cooking.
7. When cooking is complete, remove drawer from unit. Transfer chops to a plate. Serve warm.

Garlic Butter Pork Chops

SERVES: 4

PREP TIME: 10 minutes
COOK TIME: 20 minutes

4 pork chops
15 g coconut butter
2 g parsley
15 ml coconut oil
2 tsps. garlic, grated
Salt and black pepper, to taste

1. Mix all the seasonings, coconut oil, garlic, butter, and parsley in a bowl and coat the pork chops with it.
2. Cover the chops with foil and refrigerate to marinate for about 1 hour.
3. Insert a crisper plate in both drawers. Remove the foil and arrange 2 chops in a single layer in each drawer.
4. Select Zone 1, select ROAST, set temperature to 190°C, and set time to 20 minutes. Select MATCH COOK to match Zone 2 settings to Zone 1. Select START/PAUSE to begin cooking.
5. When the Zone 1 and 2 times reach 10 minutes, press START/PAUSE to pause the unit. Remove the drawers from unit and flip the chops over. Reinsert drawers in unit and press START/PAUSE to resume cooking.
6. When cooking is complete, transfer pork chops to a plate. Serve warm.

Simple Pulled Pork

SERVES: 1

PREP TIME: 5 minutes
COOK TIME: 22 minutes

25 g barbecue dry rub
450 g pork tenderloin
80 ml double cream
5 g butter

1. Massage the dry rub into the tenderloin, coating it well.
2. Install a crisper plate in Zone 1 drawer. Place tenderloin in the drawer, then insert drawer in unit.
3. Select Zone 1, select AIR FRY, set temperature to 190°C, and set time to 22 minutes. Press the START/PAUSE button to begin cooking.
4. With 5 minutes remaining, press START/PAUSE to pause the unit. Remove the drawer from unit and shred with two forks. Add the double cream and butter into the drawer along with the shredded pork. Reinsert drawer in unit and press START/PAUSE to resume cooking.
5. When cooking is complete, remove drawer from unit. Transfer shredded pork to a plate. Allow to cool, then serve.

Bacon Wrapped Pork with Apple Gravy

SERVES: 4

PREP TIME: 10 minutes
COOK TIME: 25 minutes

For the Pork:
15 g Dijon mustard
1 pork tenderloin
3 rashers of bacon
For the Apple Gravy:
45 ml ghee, divided

1 small shallot, chopped
2 apples
8 g almond flour
240 ml vegetable broth
½ tsp. Dijon mustard

1. Spread Dijon mustard all over tenderloin and wrap with rashers of bacon.
2. Install a crisper plate in Zone 1 drawer. Place wrapped pork in the drawer, then insert drawer in unit.
3. Select Zone 1, select AIR FRY, set temperature to 190°C, and set time to 20 minutes. Press the START/PAUSE button to begin cooking.
4. With 10 minutes remaining, press START/PAUSE to pause the unit. Remove the drawer from unit and flip the pork over. Reinsert drawer in unit and press START/PAUSE to resume cooking.
5. To make sauce, heat 15 ml ghee in a pan and add shallots. Cook for 1 minute.
6. Then add apples, cooking for 4 minutes until softened.
7. Add flour and 30 ml ghee to make a roux. Add broth and mustard, stirring well to combine.
8. When sauce starts to bubble, add 240 g of sautéed apples, cooking until sauce thickens.
9. Once pork tenderloin is cooked, remove drawer from unit. Allow to sit 8 minutes to rest before slicing.
10. Serve topped with apple gravy.

Teriyaki Pork and Mushroom Rolls

SERVES: 6

PREP TIME: 10 minutes
COOK TIME: 17 minutes

50 g brown sugar
60 ml mirin
60 ml soy sauce
3 g almond flour
5-cm ginger, chopped
6 (110 g) pork belly slices
170 g Enoki mushrooms

1. Mix the brown sugar, mirin, soy sauce, almond flour, and ginger together until brown sugar dissolves.
2. Take pork belly slices and wrap around a bundle of mushrooms. Brush each roll with teriyaki sauce. Chill for half an hour.
3. Insert a crisper plate in both drawers. Place 3 rolls in a single layer in each drawer.
4. Select Zone 1, select AIR FRY, set temperature to 190°C, and set time to 17 minutes. Select MATCH COOK to match Zone 2 settings to Zone 1. Select START/PAUSE to begin cooking.
5. When the Zone 1 and 2 times reach 8 minutes, press START/PAUSE to pause the unit. Remove the drawers from unit and flip the rolls over. Reinsert drawers in unit and press START/PAUSE to resume cooking.
6. When cooking is complete, transfer rolls to a plate. Serve warm.

Potato and Prosciutto Salad

SERVES: 8

PREP TIME: 10 minutes
COOK TIME: 35 minutes

For the Salad:
1.8 kg potatoes, boiled and cubed
15 slices prosciutto, diced
225 g shredded Cheddar cheese
For the Dressing:
425 g sour cream
30 ml mayonnaise
1 tsp. salt
1 tsp. black pepper
1 tsp. dried basil

1. Mix the potatoes, prosciutto, and Cheddar in a large bowl.
2. In a separate bowl, mix the sour cream, mayonnaise, salt, pepper, and basil using a whisk.
3. Insert a crisper plate in both drawers. Place half of potato mixture in a single layer in each drawer.
4. Select Zone 1, select AIR FRY, set temperature to 200°C, and set time to 35 minutes. Select MATCH COOK to match Zone 2 settings to Zone 1. Select START/PAUSE to begin cooking.
5. When the Zone 1 and 2 times reach 15 minutes, press START/PAUSE to pause the unit. Remove the drawers from unit and shake for 10 seconds. Reinsert drawers in unit and press START/PAUSE to resume cooking.
6. When cooking is complete, transfer salad to a plate. Serve warm with the dressing.

Cheese Crusted Chops

SERVES: 6

PREP TIME: 10 minutes
COOK TIME: 18 minutes

¼ tsp. pepper
½ tsp. salt
6 thick boneless pork chops
80 g pork rind crumbs
¼ tsp. chilli powder
½ tsp. onion powder
1 tsp. smoked paprika
2 beaten eggs
30 g grated Parmesan cheese
Cooking spray

1. Rub the pepper and salt on both sides of pork chops.
2. In a food processor, pulse pork rinds into crumbs. Mix crumbs with chilli powder, onion powder, and paprika in a bowl.
3. Beat eggs in another bowl.
4. Dip pork chops into eggs then into pork rind crumb mixture.
5. Insert a crisper plate in both drawers. Place 3 pork chops in a single layer in each drawer. Spritz with cooking spray.
6. Select Zone 1, select AIR FRY, set temperature to 190°C, and set time to 18 minutes. Select MATCH COOK to match Zone 2 settings to Zone 1. Select START/PAUSE to begin cooking.
7. When the Zone 1 and 2 times reach 9 minutes, press START/PAUSE to pause the unit. Remove the drawers from unit and flip the pork chops over. Reinsert drawers in unit and press START/PAUSE to resume cooking.
8. When cooking is complete, transfer pork chops to a plate. Serve warm.

Pork with Aloha Salsa

SERVES: 4

PREP TIME: 20 minutes
COOK TIME: 14 minutes

2 eggs
30 ml milk
30 g flour
30 g panko bread crumbs
12 g sesame seeds
450 g boneless, thin pork cutlets
(9-12mm thick)
Lemon pepper and salt, to taste
30 g cornflour
Cooking spray

For the Aloha Salsa:
160 g fresh pineapple, chopped in small pieces
30 g red onion, finely chopped
30 g green or red bell pepper, chopped
½ tsp. ground cinnamon
5 ml low-sodium soy sauce
⅛ tsp. crushed red pepper
⅛ tsp. ground black pepper

1. In a medium bowl, stir together all ingredients for salsa. Cover and refrigerate while cooking the pork.
2. Beat the eggs and milk in a shallow dish.
3. In another shallow dish, mix the flour, panko, and sesame seeds.
4. Sprinkle pork cutlets with lemon pepper and salt.
5. Dip pork cutlets in cornflour, egg mixture, and then panko coating. Spray both sides with cooking spray.
6. Install a crisper plate in Zone 1 drawer. Place pork cutlets in the drawer, then insert drawer in unit.
7. Select Zone 1, select AIR FRY, set temperature to 190°C, and set time to 14 minutes. Press the START/PAUSE button to begin cooking.
8. With 7 minutes remaining, press START/PAUSE to pause the unit. Remove the drawer from unit and flip the pork cutlets over. Reinsert drawer in unit and press START/PAUSE to resume cooking.
9. When cooking is complete, remove drawer from unit. Transfer pork cutlets to a plate.
10. Serve fried cutlets with salsa on the side.

Filling Pork Chops

SERVES: 2

PREP TIME: 20 minutes
COOK TIME: 15 minutes

2 (2.5-cm thick) pork chops
½ tbsp. fresh coriander, chopped
½ tbsp. fresh rosemary, chopped
½ tbsp. fresh parsley, chopped
2 garlic cloves, minced
30 ml olive oil
¾ tbsp. Dijon mustard
1 tbsp. ground coriander
5 g coconut sugar
Salt, to taste

1. Mix all the ingredients in a large bowl except the chops.
2. Coat the pork chops with marinade generously and cover to refrigerate for about 3 hours.
3. Keep the pork chops at room temperature for about 30 minutes.
4. Install a crisper plate in Zone 1 drawer. Place pork chops in the drawer, then insert drawer in unit.
5. Select Zone 1, select ROAST, set temperature to 190°C, and set time to 15 minutes. Press the START/PAUSE button to begin cooking.
6. With 7 minutes remaining, press START/PAUSE to pause the unit. Remove the drawer from unit and flip the chops over. Reinsert drawer in unit and press START/PAUSE to resume cooking.
7. When cooking is complete, remove drawer from unit. Transfer chops to a plate. Serve warm.

Caramelised Pork

SERVES: 6

PREP TIME: 10 minutes
COOK TIME: 18 minutes

900 g pork shoulder, cut into 4-cm thick slices
80 ml soy sauce
30 g sugar
15 ml honey

1. Mix all the ingredients in a large bowl and coat chops well.
2. Cover and refrigerate for about 8 hours.
3. Insert a crisper plate in both drawers. Place half of pork in each drawer.
4. Select Zone 1, select ROAST, set temperature to 190°C, and set time to 18 minutes. Select MATCH COOK to match Zone 2 settings to Zone 1. Select START/PAUSE to begin cooking.
5. When the Zone 1 and 2 times reach 9 minutes, press START/PAUSE to pause the unit. Remove the drawers from unit and flip the pork over. Reinsert drawers in unit and press START/PAUSE to resume cooking.
6. When cooking is complete, transfer pork to a plate. Serve warm.

CHAPTER 5

BEEF RECIPES

Super Simple Steaks

SERVES: 2

PREP TIME: 5 minutes
COOK TIME: 14 minutes

225 g quality cuts steak
Salt and black pepper, to taste

1. Season the steaks evenly with salt and black pepper.
2. Install a crisper plate in Zone 1 drawer. Place steaks in the drawer, then insert drawer in unit.
3. Select Zone 1, select AIR FRY, set temperature to 200°C, and set time to 14 minutes. Press the START/PAUSE button to begin cooking.
4. With 7 minutes remaining, press START/PAUSE to pause the unit. Remove the drawer from unit and flip the steaks over. Reinsert drawer in unit and press START/PAUSE to resume cooking.
5. When cooking is complete, remove drawer from unit. Transfer steaks to a plate. Serve warm.

Beef Meatballs

SERVES: 5

PREP TIME: 5 minutes
COOK TIME: 16 minutes

450 g minced beef
60 g grated Parmesan cheese
1 tbsp. minced garlic
50 g Mozzarella cheese
1 tsp. freshly ground pepper

1. In a bowl, mix all the ingredients together.
2. Roll the meat mixture into 5 generous meatballs.
3. Install a crisper plate in Zone 1 drawer. Place meatballs in the drawer, then insert drawer in unit.
4. Select Zone 1, select AIR FRY, set temperature to 200°C, and set time to 16 minutes. Press the START/PAUSE button to begin cooking.
5. With 8 minutes remaining, press START/PAUSE to pause the unit. Remove the drawer from unit and flip the meatballs over. Reinsert drawer in unit and press START/PAUSE to resume cooking.
6. When cooking is complete, remove drawer from unit. Transfer meatballs to a plate. Serve warm.

Rosemary Ribeye Steaks

SERVES: 2

PREP TIME: 10 minutes
COOK TIME: 16 minutes

30 g butter
1 clove garlic, minced
Salt and ground black pepper, to taste
22 ml balsamic vinegar
5 g rosemary, chopped
2 ribeye steaks

1. Melt the butter in a frying pan over medium heat. Add the garlic and fry until fragrant.
2. Remove the frying pan from the heat and add the salt, pepper, and vinegar. Allow it to cool.
3. Add the rosemary, then pour the mixture into a Ziploc bag.
4. Put the ribeye steaks in the bag and shake well, coating the meat well. Refrigerate for an hour, then allow to sit for a further 20 minutes.
5. Install a crisper plate in Zone 1 drawer. Place ribeyes in the drawer, then insert drawer in unit.
6. Select Zone 1, select AIR FRY, set temperature to 200°C, and set time to 16 minutes. Press the START/PAUSE button to begin cooking.
7. With 8 minutes remaining, press START/PAUSE to pause the unit. Remove the drawer from unit and flip the ribeyes over. Reinsert drawer in unit and press START/PAUSE to resume cooking.
8. When cooking is complete, remove drawer from unit. Transfer ribeyes to a plate. Serve warm.

Bacon-Wrapped Beef Hot Dog

SERVES: 4

PREP TIME: 5 minutes
COOK TIME: 12 minutes

4 rashers of sugar-free bacon
4 beef hot dogs

1. Take a rasher of bacon and wrap it around the hot dog, securing it with a toothpick. Repeat with the other pieces of bacon and hot dogs.
2. Install a crisper plate in Zone 1 drawer. Place wrapped dogs in the drawer, then insert drawer in unit.
3. Select Zone 1, select AIR FRY, set temperature to 200°C, and set time to 12 minutes. Press the START/PAUSE button to begin cooking.
4. With 6 minutes remaining, press START/PAUSE to pause the unit. Remove the drawer from unit and flip the wrapped dogs over. Reinsert drawer in unit and press START/PAUSE to resume cooking.
5. When cooking is complete, remove drawer from unit. Transfer wrapped dogs to a plate. Serve warm.

Smoky Beef Burgers

SERVES: 4

PREP TIME: 20 minutes
COOK TIME: 12 minutes

450 g minced beef
4 whole-wheat hamburger buns, split and toasted
15 ml Worcestershire sauce
5 ml Maggi seasoning sauce
3-4 drops liquid smoke
1 tsp. dried parsley
½ tsp. garlic powder
½ tsp. onion powder
Salt and ground black pepper, as required

1. Mix the beef, sauces, liquid smoke, parsley, and spices in a bowl.
2. Make 4 equal-sized patties from the beef mixture.
3. Insert a crisper plate in both drawers. Place 2 patties in a single layer in each drawer.
4. Select Zone 1, select AIR FRY, set temperature to 190°C, and set time to 12 minutes. Select MATCH COOK to match Zone 2 settings to Zone 1. Select START/PAUSE to begin cooking.
5. When the Zone 1 and 2 times reach 6 minutes, press START/PAUSE to pause the unit. Remove the drawers from unit and flip the patties over. Reinsert drawers in unit and press START/PAUSE to resume cooking.
6. When cooking is complete, transfer patties to a plate. Serve on a bun.

Buttered Filet Mignon

SERVES: 4

PREP TIME: 10 minutes
COOK TIME: 15 minutes

2 (170 g) filet mignon steaks
15 g butter, softened
Salt and black pepper, to taste

1. Rub the steak generously with salt and black pepper and coat with butter.
2. Install a crisper plate in Zone 1 drawer. Place the steaks in the drawer, then insert drawer in unit.
3. Select Zone 1, select ROAST, set temperature to 200°C, and set time to 15 minutes. Press the START/PAUSE button to begin cooking.
4. With 7 minutes remaining, press START/PAUSE to pause the unit. Remove the drawer from unit and flip the steaks over. Reinsert drawer in unit and press START/PAUSE to resume cooking.
5. When cooking is complete, remove drawer from unit. Transfer the steaks to a plate and cut into desired size slices to serve.

Herbed Beef Roast

SERVES: 5

PREP TIME: 10 minutes
COOK TIME: 45 minutes

900 g beef roast
15 ml olive oil
1 tsp. dried rosemary, crushed
1 tsp. dried thyme, crushed
Salt, to taste

1. Rub the roast generously with herb mixture and coat with olive oil.
2. Install a crisper plate in Zone 1 drawer. Place the roast in the drawer, then insert drawer in unit.
3. Select Zone 1, select ROAST, set temperature to 200°C, and set time to 45 minutes. Press the START/PAUSE button to begin cooking.
4. With 20 minutes remaining, press START/PAUSE to pause the unit. Remove the drawer from unit and flip the roast over. Reinsert drawer in unit and press START/PAUSE to resume cooking.
5. When cooking is complete, remove drawer from unit. Transfer the roast to a plate. Cut into desired size slices and serve.

Beef Loin with Thyme and Parsley

SERVES: 4

PREP TIME: 5 minutes
COOK TIME: 15 minutes

15 g butter, melted
¼ tsp. dried thyme
1 tsp. garlic salt
¼ tsp. dried parsley
450 g beef loin

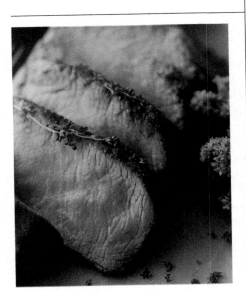

1. In a bowl, combine the melted butter, thyme, garlic salt, and parsley.
2. Cut the beef loin into slices and generously apply the seasoned butter using a brush.
3. Install a crisper plate in Zone 1 drawer. Place beef loin in the drawer, then insert drawer in unit.
4. Select Zone 1, select AIR FRY, set temperature to 200°C, and set time to 15 minutes. Press the START/PAUSE button to begin cooking.
5. With 7 minutes remaining, press START/PAUSE to pause the unit. Remove the drawer from unit and flip the beef loin over. Reinsert drawer in unit and press START/PAUSE to resume cooking.
6. When cooking is complete, remove drawer from unit. Transfer beef loin to a plate. Serve warm.

Classic Spring Rolls

SERVES: 20

PREP TIME: 10 minutes
COOK TIME: 10 minutes

30 g noodles
220 g minced beef
5 ml soy sauce
140 g fresh mix vegetables
3 garlic cloves, minced

1 small onion, diced
15 ml sesame oil
1 packet spring roll sheets
30 ml cold water

1. Cook the noodles in enough hot water to soften them up, drain them and snip them to make them shorter.
2. In a frying pan over medium heat, cook the beef, soy sauce, mixed vegetables, garlic, and onion in sesame oil until the beef is cooked through. Take the pan off the heat and throw in the noodles. Mix well to incorporate everything.
3. Unroll a spring roll sheet and lay it flat. Scatter the filling diagonally across it and roll it up, brushing the edges lightly with water to act as an adhesive. Repeat until you have used up all the sheets and the filling.
4. Coat each spring roll with a light brushing of oil.
5. Insert a crisper plate in both drawers. Place half of the spring rolls in a single layer in each drawer.
6. Select Zone 1, select AIR FRY, set temperature to 180°C, and set time to 10 minutes. Select MATCH COOK to match Zone 2 settings to Zone 1. Select START/PAUSE to begin cooking.
7. When the Zone 1 and 2 times reach 5 minutes, press START/PAUSE to pause the unit. Remove the drawers from unit and flip the spring rolls over. Reinsert drawers in unit and press START/PAUSE to resume cooking.
8. When cooking is complete, transfer spring rolls to a plate. Serve hot.

Beef Steak Fingers

SERVES: 4

PREP TIME: 5 minutes
COOK TIME: 12 minutes

4 small beef cube steaks
Salt and ground black pepper, to taste
50 g whole wheat flour
Cooking spray

1. Cut cube steaks into 2.5-cm-wide strips.
2. Sprinkle lightly with salt and pepper to taste.
3. Roll in flour to coat all sides.
4. Insert a crisper plate in both drawers. Place half of steak strips in a single layer in each drawer. Spritz steak strips with cooking spray.
5. Select Zone 1, select AIR FRY, set temperature to 200°C, and set time to 12 minutes. Select MATCH COOK to match Zone 2 settings to Zone 1. Select START/PAUSE to begin cooking.
6. When the Zone 1 and 2 times reach 6 minutes, press START/PAUSE to pause the unit. Remove the drawers from unit and flip the steak strips over. Spritz with cooking spray. Reinsert drawers in unit and press START/PAUSE to resume cooking.
7. When cooking is complete, steak fingers should be crispy outside with no red juices inside. Transfer to a plate and serve warm.

Beef and Vegetable Cubes

SERVES: 4

PREP TIME: 15 minutes
COOK TIME: 18 minutes

30 ml olive oil
15 ml apple cider vinegar
1 tsp. fine sea salt
½ tsp. ground black pepper
1 tsp. shallot powder
¾ tsp. smoked cayenne pepper
½ tsp. garlic powder
¼ tsp. ground cumin
450 g top round steak, cut into cubes
115 g broccoli, cut into florets
115 g mushrooms, sliced
1 tsp. dried basil
1 tsp. celery seeds

1. Massage the olive oil, vinegar, salt, black pepper, shallot powder, cayenne pepper, garlic powder, and cumin into the cubed steak, ensuring to coat each piece evenly.
2. Allow to marinate for a minimum of 3 hours.
3. Insert a crisper plate in both drawers. Place beef cubes in the Zone 1 drawer, then insert drawer in unit. Place vegetables in the Zone 2 drawer along with basil and celery seeds, then insert drawer in unit.
4. Select Zone 1, select AIR FRY, set temperature to 200°C, and set time to 14 minutes. Select Zone 2, select AIR FRY, set temperature to 200°C, and set time to 18 minutes. Select SYNC. Press the START/PAUSE button to begin cooking.
5. When the Zone 1 and 2 times reach 7 minutes, press START/PAUSE to pause the unit. Remove the drawers from unit and shake for 10 seconds. Reinsert drawers in unit and press START/PAUSE to resume cooking.
6. When cooking is complete, serve beef cubes with vegetables.

Beef Cheeseburger Egg Rolls

MAKES 6 EGG ROLLS

PREP TIME: 15 minutes
COOK TIME: 10 minutes

225 g raw lean beef, minced
60 g chopped onion
60 g chopped bell pepper
¼ tsp. onion powder
¼ tsp. garlic powder
45 g cream cheese
1 tbsp. yellow mustard
21 g shredded Cheddar cheese
6 chopped dill gherkin slices
6 egg roll wrappers

1. In a frying pan, add the beef, onion, bell pepper, onion powder, and garlic powder. Stir and crumble beef until fully cooked, and vegetables are soft.
2. Take frying pan off the heat and add cream cheese, mustard, and Cheddar cheese, stirring until melted.
3. Pour beef mixture into a bowl and fold in gherkins.
4. Lay out egg wrappers and divide the beef mixture into each one. Moisten egg roll wrapper edges with water. Fold sides to the middle and seal with water. Repeat with all other egg rolls.
5. Insert a crisper plate in both drawers. Place half of the rolls in a single layer in each drawer.
6. Select Zone 1, select AIR FRY, set temperature to 200°C, and set time to 10 minutes. Select MATCH COOK to match Zone 2 settings to Zone 1. Select START/PAUSE to begin cooking.
7. When cooking is complete, transfer the rolls to a plate. Serve hot.

Holiday Spicy Beef Roast

SERVES: 8

PREP TIME: 10 minutes
COOK TIME: 40 minutes

900 g roast beef, at room temperature
30 ml extra-virgin olive oil
1 tsp. sea salt flakes
1 tsp. black pepper, preferably freshly ground
1 tsp. smoked paprika
A few dashes of liquid smoke
2 jalapeño peppers, thinly sliced

1. Pat the roast dry using kitchen towels. Rub with extra-virgin olive oil and all seasonings along with liquid smoke.
2. Install a crisper plate in Zone 1 drawer. Place the roast in the drawer, then insert drawer in unit.
3. Select Zone 1, select AIR FRY, set temperature to 200°C, and set time to 40 minutes. Press the START/PAUSE button to begin cooking.
4. With 20 minutes remaining, press START/PAUSE to pause the unit. Remove the drawer from unit and flip the roast over. Reinsert drawer in unit and press START/PAUSE to resume cooking.
5. When cooking is complete, remove drawer from unit. Transfer roast to a plate. Serve sprinkled with sliced jalapeños. Bon appétit!

Mozzarella Beef Brisket

SERVES: 6

PREP TIME: 5 minutes
COOK TIME: 25 minutes

340 g beef brisket
2 tsps. Italian herbs
10 ml olive oil
1 onion, sliced
200 g Mozzarella cheese, sliced

1. Cut up the brisket into four equal slices and season with the Italian herbs.
2. Drizzle the slices of beef with olive oil.
3. Install a crisper plate in Zone 1 drawer. Place the brisket slices in the drawer along with the onion, then insert drawer in unit.
4. Select Zone 1, select AIR FRY, set temperature to 180°C, and set time to 25 minutes. Press the START/PAUSE button to begin cooking.
5. With 5 minutes remaining, press START/PAUSE to pause the unit. Remove the drawer from unit and put a piece of Mozzarella on top of each piece of brisket. Reinsert drawer in unit and press START/PAUSE to resume cooking.
6. When cooking is complete, remove drawer from unit. Transfer brisket slices to a plate. Serve warm.

CHAPTER 6
POULTRY RECIPES

Spinach Stuffed Chicken Breasts

SERVES: 2

PREP TIME: 15 minutes
COOK TIME: 29 minutes

50 g fresh spinach
30 g ricotta cheese, shredded
2 (115 g) skinless, boneless chicken breasts
20 g cheddar cheese, grated
15 ml olive oil
Salt and ground black pepper, as required
¼ tsp. paprika

1. Heat olive oil in a medium frying pan over medium heat and cook spinach for about 4 minutes.
2. Add the ricotta and cook for about 1 minute.
3. Cut the slits in each chicken breast horizontally and stuff with the spinach mixture.
4. Season each chicken breast evenly with salt and black pepper and top with cheddar cheese and paprika.
5. Install a crisper plate in Zone 1 drawer. Place chicken breasts in the drawer, then insert drawer in unit.
6. Select Zone 1, select AIR FRY, set temperature to 190°C, and set time to 25 minutes. Press the START/PAUSE button to begin cooking.
7. When cooking is complete, remove drawer from unit. Transfer chicken breasts to a plate. Serve warm.

Succulent Duck Breast with Balsamic Vinaigrette

SERVES: 2

PREP TIME: 15 minutes
COOK TIME: 20 minutes

2 g fresh thyme, chopped
1 (300 g) duck breast
4 cherry tomatoes
40 g black olives
15 ml olive oil
5 ml mustard
240 ml beer
Salt and freshly ground black pepper, to taste
15 ml balsamic vinegar

1. Mix olive oil, mustard, thyme, beer, salt and black pepper in a bowl.
2. Add duck breast and coat generously with marinade.
3. Cover the duck breast with foil paper and refrigerate for about 4 hours.
4. Insert a crisper plate in both drawers. Place duck breast in the Zone 1 drawer, then insert drawer in unit. Place tomatoes in the Zone 2 drawer, then insert drawer in unit.
5. Select Zone 1, select ROAST, set temperature to 200°C, and set time to 25 minutes. Select Zone 2, select ROAST, set temperature to 200°C, and set time to 15 minutes. Select SYNC. Press the START/PAUSE button to begin cooking.
6. When the Zone 1 and 2 times reach 10 minutes, press START/PAUSE to pause the unit. Remove the drawers from unit and flip the duck breast and cherry tomatoes over. Reinsert drawers in unit and press START/PAUSE to resume cooking.
7. When cooking is complete, transfer the duck and tomatoes to a plate. Drizzle with vinegar and serve topped with olives.

Spicy Chicken Legs

SERVES: 3

PREP TIME: 15 minutes
COOK TIME: 22 minutes

3 (225 g) chicken legs
240 ml buttermilk
220 g white flour
1 tsp. garlic powder
1 tsp. onion powder
1 tsp. ground cumin
1 tsp. paprika
Salt and ground black pepper, as required
15 ml olive oil

1. Mix the chicken legs, and buttermilk in a bowl and refrigerate for about 2 hours.
2. Combine the flour and spices in another bowl and dredge the chicken legs into this mixture.
3. Now, dip the chicken into the buttermilk and coat again with the flour mixture.
4. Install a crisper plate in Zone 1 drawer. Place chicken legs in the drawer and drizzle with the oil, then insert drawer in unit.
5. Select Zone 1, select ROAST, set temperature to 200°C, and set time to 22 minutes. Press the START/PAUSE button to begin cooking.
6. With 10 minutes remaining, press START/PAUSE to pause the unit. Remove the drawer from unit and flip the chicken legs over. Reinsert drawer in unit and press START/PAUSE to resume cooking.
7. When cooking is complete, remove drawer from unit. Transfer chicken legs to a plate. Serve warm.

Gingered Chicken Drumsticks

SERVES: 3

PREP TIME: 10 minutes
COOK TIME: 22 minutes

60 ml full-fat coconut milk
3 (170 g) chicken drumsticks
2 tsps. fresh ginger, minced
2 tsps. galangal, minced
2 tsps. ground turmeric
Salt, to taste

1. Mix the coconut milk, galangal, ginger, and spices in a bowl.
2. Add the chicken drumsticks and coat generously with the marinade.
3. Refrigerate to marinate for at least 8 hours.
4. Install a crisper plate in Zone 1 drawer. Place chicken drumsticks in the drawer, then insert drawer in unit.
5. Select Zone 1, select AIR FRY, set temperature to 200°C, and set time to 22 minutes. Press the START/PAUSE button to begin cooking.
6. With 10 minutes remaining, press START/PAUSE to pause the unit. Remove the drawer from unit and flip the chicken drumsticks over. Reinsert drawer in unit and press START/PAUSE to resume cooking.
7. When cooking is complete, remove drawer from unit. Transfer chicken drumsticks to a plate. Serve warm.

Deliciously Crisp Chicken

SERVES: 4

PREP TIME: 10 minutes
COOK TIME: 28 minutes

1 egg, beaten
60 g breadcrumbs
8 skinless, boneless chicken tenderloins
30 ml vegetable oil

1. Whisk the egg in a shallow dish and mix vegetable oil and breadcrumbs in another shallow dish.
2. Dip the chicken tenderloins in egg and then coat in the breadcrumb mixture.
3. Insert a crisper plate in both drawers. Place 4 chicken tenderloins in a single layer in each drawer.
4. Select Zone 1, select ROAST, set temperature to 200°C, and set time to 28 minutes. Select MATCH COOK to match Zone 2 settings to Zone 1. Select START/PAUSE to begin cooking.
5. When the Zone 1 and 2 times reach 14 minutes, press START/PAUSE to pause the unit. Remove the drawers from unit and flip the chicken tenderloins over. Reinsert drawers in unit and press START/PAUSE to resume cooking.
6. When cooking is complete, transfer chicken tenderloins to a plate. Serve warm.

Sweet Chicken Kebabs

SERVES: 3

PREP TIME: 20 minutes
COOK TIME: 15 minutes

4 spring onions, chopped
8 g sesame seeds, toasted
450 g chicken tenders
Wooden skewers, presoaked
6 g fresh ginger, finely grated

4 garlic cloves, minced
120 ml pineapple juice
120 ml soy sauce
60 ml sesame oil
A pinch of black pepper

1. Mix scallion, ginger, garlic, pineapple juice, soy sauce, oil, sesame seeds, and black pepper in a large baking dish.
2. Thread chicken tenders onto pre-soaked wooden skewers.
3. Coat the skewers generously with marinade and refrigerate for about 2 hours.
4. Insert a crisper plate in both drawers. Place half of the skewers in a single layer in each drawer.
5. Select Zone 1, select ROAST, set temperature to 190°C, and set time to 15 minutes. Select MATCH COOK to match Zone 2 settings to Zone 1. Select START/PAUSE to begin cooking.
6. When the Zone 1 and 2 times reach 8 minutes, press START/PAUSE to pause the unit. Remove the drawers from unit and flip the skewers over. Reinsert drawers in unit and press START/PAUSE to resume cooking.
7. When cooking is complete, transfer skewers to a plate. Serve warm.

Roasted Chicken with Potatoes

SERVES: 2

PREP TIME: 15 minutes
COOK TIME: 40 minutes

1 (680 g) whole chicken
225 g small potatoes
Salt and black pepper, as required
15 ml olive oil

1. Season the chicken and potatoes with salt and black pepper and drizzle with olive oil.
2. Insert a crisper plate in both drawers. Place chicken in the Zone 1 drawer, then insert drawer in unit. Place potatoes in the Zone 2 drawer, then insert drawer in unit.
3. Select Zone 1, select ROAST, set temperature to 200°C, and set time to 40 minutes. Select Zone 2, select AIR FRY, set temperature to 200°C, and set time to 30 minutes. Select SYNC. Press the START/ PAUSE button to begin cooking.
4. When the Zone 1 and Zone 2 times reach 15 minutes, press START/ PAUSE and remove drawers from unit. In Zone 1, flip the chicken over. In Zone 2, shake for 10 seconds. Reinsert drawers in unit and press START/PAUSE to resume cooking.
5. When cooking is complete, serve chicken with potatoes.

Tandoori Chicken Legs

SERVES: 4

PREP TIME: 15 minutes
COOK TIME: 22 minutes

4 chicken legs
4 tbsps. hung curd
45 ml fresh lemon juice
3 tsps. ginger paste
3 tsps. garlic paste
Salt, as required
2 tbsps. tandoori masala powder

2 tsps. red chilli powder
1 tsp. garam masala powder
1 tsp. ground cumin
1 tsp. ground coriander
1 tsp. ground turmeric
Ground black pepper, as required
Pinch of orange food colour

1. Mix chicken legs, lemon juice, ginger paste, garlic paste, and salt in a bowl.
2. Combine the curd, spices, and food colour in another bowl.
3. Add the chicken legs into bowl and coat generously with the spice mixture.
4. Cover the bowl of chicken and refrigerate for at least 12 hours.
5. Install a crisper plate in Zone 1 drawer. Place chicken legs in the drawer, then insert drawer in unit.
6. Select Zone 1, select ROAST, set temperature to 200°C, and set time to 22 minutes. Press the START/PAUSE button to begin cooking.
7. With 10 minutes remaining, press START/PAUSE to pause the unit. Remove the drawer from unit and flip the chicken legs over. Reinsert drawer in unit and press START/PAUSE to resume cooking.
8. When cooking is complete, remove drawer from unit. Transfer chicken legs to a plate. Serve warm.

(Note: Hung curd - Hung curd is nothing but yoghurt drained of all its water. It can be made very easily at home.)

Cheese Stuffed Turkey Breasts

SERVES: 4

PREP TIME: 15 minutes
COOK TIME: 20 minutes

2 (225 g) turkey breast fillets, skinless and boneless, each cut into 2 pieces
4 cheddar cheese slices
2 g fresh parsley, minced
4 rashers of bacon
Salt and black pepper, to taste

1. Make a slit in each turkey piece horizontally and season with salt and black pepper.
2. Insert cheddar cheese slice into the slits and sprinkle with parsley.
3. Wrap each turkey piece with one rasher of bacon.
4. Install a crisper plate in Zone 1 drawer. Place turkey pieces in the drawer, then insert drawer in unit.
5. Select Zone 1, select AIR FRY, set temperature to 200°C, and set time to 20 minutes. Press the START/PAUSE button to begin cooking.
6. With 10 minutes remaining, press START/PAUSE to pause the unit. Remove the drawer from unit and flip the turkey pieces over. Reinsert drawer in unit and press START/PAUSE to resume cooking.
7. When cooking is complete, remove drawer from unit. Transfer turkey pieces to a plate. Serve warm.

Chicken and Veggie Kababs

SERVES: 3

PREP TIME: 20 minutes
COOK TIME: 25 minutes

450 g skinless, boneless chicken thighs, cut into cubes
120 ml plain Greek yoghurt
2 small tomatoes, seeded and cut into large chunks
1 large red onion, cut into large chunks
Wooden skewers, presoaked
15 ml olive oil
2 tsps. curry powder
½ tsp. smoked paprika
¼ tsp. cayenne pepper
Salt, to taste

1. Mix the chicken, oil, yoghurt, and spices in a large baking dish.
2. Thread chicken cubes, tomatoes and onion onto presoaked wooden skewers.
3. Coat the skewers generously with marinade and refrigerate for about 3 hours.
4. Insert a crisper plate in both drawers. Place half of the skewers in each drawer.
5. Select Zone 1, select ROAST, set temperature to 180°C, and set time to 25 minutes. Select MATCH COOK to match Zone 2 settings to Zone 1. Select START/PAUSE to begin cooking.
6. When the Zone 1 and 2 times reach 10 minutes, press START/PAUSE to pause the unit. Remove the drawers from unit and flip the skewers over. Reinsert drawers in unit and press START/PAUSE to resume cooking.
7. When cooking is complete, transfer skewers to a plate. Serve warm.

Roasted Cajun Turkey

SERVES: 4

PREP TIME: 10 minutes
COOK TIME: 30 minutes

900 g turkey thighs, skinless and boneless
1 red onion, sliced
2 bell peppers, sliced
1 bird's eye chilli, minced
1 carrot, sliced
1 tbsp. Cajun seasoning mix
15 ml fish sauce
480 ml chicken broth
Nonstick cooking spray

1. Add the turkey thighs, onion, peppers, chilli, and carrot with Cajun seasoning, fish sauce and chicken broth and mix well. Lightly spray with the cooking spray.
2. Insert a crisper plate in both drawers. Place turkey thigh in the Zone 1 drawer, then insert drawer in unit. Place vegetables in the Zone 2 drawer, then insert drawer in unit.
3. Select Zone 1, select ROAST, set temperature to 200°C, and set time to 30 minutes. Select Zone 2, select AIR FRY, set temperature to 200°C, and set time to 20 minutes. Select SYNC. Press the START/PAUSE button to begin cooking.
4. When the Zone 1 and Zone 2 times reach 10 minutes, press START/PAUSE and remove drawers from unit. In Zone 1, flip the turkey thigh. In Zone 2, shake for 10 seconds. Reinsert drawers in unit and press START/PAUSE to resume cooking.
5. When cooking is complete, serve turkey thigh with vegetables.

Sweet and Sour Chicken Thighs

SERVES: 2

PREP TIME: 15 minutes
COOK TIME: 20 minutes

1 scallion, finely chopped
2 (115 g) skinless, boneless chicken thighs
50 g corn flour
1 garlic clove, minced
7 ml soy sauce
7 ml rice vinegar
5 g sugar
Salt and black pepper, as required

1. Mix all the ingredients except chicken and corn flour in a bowl.
2. Place the corn flour in another bowl.
3. Coat the chicken thighs into the marinade and then dredge into the corn flour.
4. Install a crisper plate in Zone 1 drawer. Place chicken thighs in the drawer, skin side down, then insert drawer in unit.
5. Select Zone 1, select AIR FRY, set temperature to 200°C, and set time to 20 minutes. Press the START/PAUSE button to begin cooking.
6. With 10 minutes remaining, press START/PAUSE to pause the unit. Remove the drawer from unit and flip the chicken thighs over. Reinsert drawer in unit and press START/PAUSE to resume cooking.
7. When cooking is complete, remove drawer from unit. Transfer chicken thighs to a plate. Serve warm.

Cheesy Chicken Breasts with Courgette

SERVES: 2

PREP TIME: 20 minutes
COOK TIME: 25 minutes

2 (170 g) chicken breasts
1 egg, beaten
115 g breadcrumbs
3 g fresh basil
30 g grated Parmesan cheese, divided
30 ml vegetable oil
60 ml pasta sauce
1 small courgette, sliced into 1-cm thick rounds
15 ml olive oil, divided
2 tbsps. fat-free Italian dressing
Salt, to taste

1. Whisk egg in a bowl and mix breadcrumbs, vegetable oil and basil in another bowl.
2. Dip the chicken breasts into the egg and then coat with the breadcrumb mixture.
3. Mix courgette, 2 tbsps. Parmesan cheese, olive oil, Italian dressing, and salt in a medium bowl and toss to coat well.
4. Insert a crisper plate in both drawers. Place chicken breasts in the Zone 1 drawer, then insert drawer in unit. Place courgette slices in the Zone 2 drawer, then insert drawer in unit.
5. Select Zone 1, select AIR FRY, set temperature to 190°C, and set time to 25 minutes. Select Zone 2, select AIR FRY, set temperature to 200°C, and set time to 20 minutes. Select SYNC. Press the START/PAUSE button to begin cooking.
6. When the Zone 1 and Zone 2 times reach 10 minutes, press START/PAUSE and remove drawers from unit. In Zone 1, top the chicken breasts with pasta sauce and the remaining Parmesan cheese. In Zone 2, shake for 10 seconds. Reinsert drawers in unit and press START/PAUSE to resume cooking.
7. When cooking is complete, serve chicken breasts with courgette.

Parmesan Chicken Cutlets with Mushroom

SERVES: 4

PREP TIME: 15 minutes
COOK TIME: 30 minutes

80 g plain flour
2 large eggs
150 g panko breadcrumbs
30 g Parmesan cheese, grated
4 (170 g) (0.5-cm thick) skinless, boneless chicken cutlets

1 tbsp. mustard powder
Salt and black pepper, to taste
225 g chestnut mushrooms, halved
30 ml soy sauce
30 ml maple syrup
30 ml rice vinegar
2 garlic cloves, finely chopped

1. Place the flour in a shallow bowl and whisk the eggs in a second bowl.
2. Mix the breadcrumbs, cheese, mustard powder, salt, and black pepper in a third bowl.
3. Season the chicken with salt and black pepper and coat the chicken with flour.
4. Dip the chicken into whisked eggs and finally dredge into the breadcrumb mixture.
5. Insert a crisper plate in both drawers. Place the chicken cutlets in the Zone 1 drawer, then insert drawer in unit. Place mushrooms in the Zone 2 drawer, then insert drawer in unit.
6. Select Zone 1, select AIR FRY, set temperature to 200°C, and set time to 30 minutes. Select Zone 2, select ROAST, set temperature to 200°C, and set time to 15 minutes. Select SYNC. Press the START/PAUSE button to begin cooking.
7. Meanwhile, mix soy sauce, maple syrup, vinegar and garlic in a bowl.
8. When the Zone 1 and Zone 2 times reach 8 minutes, press START/PAUSE and remove drawers from unit. In Zone 1, flip the chicken over. In Zone 2, Spread the soy sauce mixture over the mushrooms. Reinsert drawers in unit and press START/PAUSE to resume cooking.
9. When cooking is complete, serve chicken with mushrooms.

CHAPTER 7
SNACK AND DESSERT RECIPES

Simple and Easy Croutons

SERVES: 4

PREP TIME: 5 minutes
COOK TIME: 10 minutes

2 slices friendly bread
15 ml olive oil
Hot soup, for serving

1. Cut the slices of bread into medium-size chunks.
2. Install a crisper plate in Zone 1 drawer and brush with the oil. Place the bread chunks in the drawer, then insert drawer in unit.
3. Select Zone 1, select AIR FRY, set temperature to 200°C, and set time to 10 minutes. Press the START/PAUSE button to begin cooking.
4. With 5 minutes remaining, press START/PAUSE to pause the unit. Remove the drawer from unit and shake for 10 seconds. Reinsert drawer in unit and press START/PAUSE to resume cooking.
5. When cooking is complete, remove drawer from unit. Transfer bread chunks to a plate. Serve with hot soup.

Herbed Pitta Crisps

SERVES: 4

PREP TIME: 5 minutes
COOK TIME: 6 minutes

¼ tsp. dried basil
¼ tsp. marjoram
¼ tsp. ground oregano
¼ tsp. garlic powder
¼ tsp. ground thyme
¼ tsp. salt
2 whole grain 15-cm pittas
Cooking spray

1. Mix all the seasonings together.
2. Cut each pitta half into 4 wedges. Break apart wedges at the fold.
3. Mist one side of pitta wedges with oil. Sprinkle with half of seasoning mix.
4. Turn pitta wedges over, mist the other side with oil, and sprinkle with remaining seasonings.
5. Install a crisper plate in Zone 1 drawer. Place pitta wedges in the drawer, then insert drawer in unit.
6. Select Zone 1, select AIR FRY, set temperature to 160°C, and set time to 6 minutes. Press the START/PAUSE button to begin cooking, shaking every 2 minutes.
7. When cooking is complete, remove drawer from unit. Serve hot.

Rosemary-Garlic Matchstick Fries

SERVES: 2

PREP TIME: 5 minutes
COOK TIME: 18 minutes

1 large russet potato (about 340 g), scrubbed clean, and julienned
15 ml vegetable oil
Leaves from 1 sprig fresh rosemary
Coarse salt and freshly ground black pepper, to taste
1 garlic clove, thinly sliced
Flaky sea salt, for serving

1. Place the julienned potatoes in a large colander and rinse under cold running water until the water runs clear. Spread the potatoes out on a double-thick layer of paper towels and pat dry.
2. In a large bowl, combine the potatoes, oil, and rosemary. Season with coarse salt and pepper and toss to coat evenly.
3. Install a crisper plate in Zone 1 drawer. Place potatoes in the drawer, then insert drawer in unit.
4. Select Zone 1, select AIR FRY, set temperature to 200°C, and set time to 18 minutes. Press the START/PAUSE button to begin cooking.
5. With 10 minutes remaining, press START/PAUSE to pause the unit. Remove the drawer from unit and shake for 10 seconds. Reinsert drawer in unit and press START/PAUSE to resume cooking.
6. With 5 minutes remaining, press START/PAUSE to pause the unit. Remove the drawer from unit. Shake for 10 seconds and add the garlic. Reinsert drawer in unit and press START/PAUSE to resume cooking.
7. When cooking is complete, remove drawer from unit. Transfer fries to a plate and sprinkle with flaky sea salt while they're hot. Serve immediately.

Spicy Kale Crisps

SERVES: 4

PREP TIME: 5 minutes
COOK TIME: 15 minutes

500 g kale, large stems removed and chopped
10 g rapeseed oil
¼ tsp. smoked paprika
¼ tsp. coarse salt
Cooking spray

1. In a large bowl, toss the kale, rapeseed oil, smoked paprika, and coarse salt.
2. Insert a crisper plate in both drawers. Place half the kale in each drawer. Spray with cooking spray.
3. Select Zone 1, select AIR FRY, set temperature to 150°C, and set time to 15 minutes. Select MATCH COOK to match Zone 2 settings to Zone 1. Select START/PAUSE to begin cooking.
4. When the Zone 1 and 2 times reach 8 minutes, press START/PAUSE to pause the unit. Remove the drawers from unit and shake for 10 seconds. Reinsert drawers in unit and press START/PAUSE to resume cooking.
5. When cooking is complete, transfer kale to a plate and allow to cool on a wire rack for 3 to 5 minutes before serving.

Crispy Prosciutto-Wrapped Asparagus

SERVES: 6

PREP TIME: 5 minutes
COOK TIME: 20 minutes

12 asparagus spears, woody ends trimmed
24 pieces thinly sliced prosciutto
Cooking spray

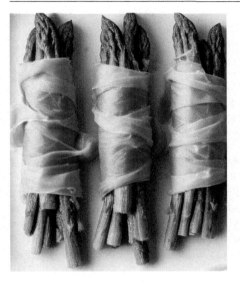

1. Wrap each asparagus spear with 2 slices of prosciutto, then repeat this process with the remaining asparagus and prosciutto.
2. Insert a crisper plate in both drawers. Place 3 bundles in a single layer in each drawer. Spray with cooking spray.
3. Select Zone 1, select AIR FRY, set temperature to 200°C, and set time to 10 minutes. Select MATCH COOK to match Zone 2 settings to Zone 1. Select START/PAUSE to begin cooking. Repeat this process with the remaining asparagus bundles.
4. Remove the bundles and allow to cool on a wire rack for 5 minutes before serving.

Chocolate Molten Cake

SERVES: 4

PREP TIME: 5 minutes
COOK TIME: 12 minutes

100 g butter, melted
45 g sugar
100 g chocolate, melted
12 g flour
2 eggs

1. Grease four 7-cm ramekins with a little butter.
2. Rigorously combine the eggs, butter, and sugar before stirring in the melted chocolate.
3. Slowly fold in the flour.
4. Spoon an equal amount of the mixture into each ramekin.
5. Insert a crisper plate in both drawers. Place 2 ramekins in each drawer.
6. Select Zone 1, select BAKE, set temperature to 190°C, and set time to 12 minutes. Select MATCH COOK to match Zone 2 settings to Zone 1. Select START/PAUSE to begin cooking.
7. When cooking is complete, put the ramekins upside-down on plates and let the cakes fall out. Serve hot.

Chocolate Yoghurt Pecans Muffins

SERVES: 8

PREP TIME: 15 minutes
COOK TIME: 12 minutes

180 g plain flour
10 g baking powder
240 ml yoghurt
45 g mini chocolate chips
30 g pecans, chopped
50 g sugar
½ tsp. salt
80 ml vegetable oil
2 tsps. vanilla extract

1. Grease 8 muffin moulds lightly.
2. Mix flour, sugar, baking powder, and salt in a bowl.
3. Mix the yoghurt, oil, and vanilla extract in another bowl.
4. Fold in the chocolate chips and pecans and divide the mixture evenly into the muffin moulds.
5. Insert a crisper plate in both drawers. Place 4 muffin moulds in a single layer in each drawer.
6. Select Zone 1, select BAKE, set temperature to 180°C, and set time to 12 minutes. Select MATCH COOK to match Zone 2 settings to Zone 1. Select START/PAUSE to begin cooking.
7. When cooking is complete, remove the muffin moulds from Air fryer and invert the muffins onto wire rack to cool completely before serving.

Shortbread Fingers

SERVES: 10

PREP TIME: 10 minutes
COOK TIME: 14 minutes

cooking spray
200 g plain flour
170 g butter
60 g caster sugar

1. Mix sugar, flour and butter in a bowl to form a dough.
2. Cut the dough into 10 equal sized fingers and prick the fingers lightly with a fork.
3. Insert a crisper plate in both drawer and spray with cooking spray. Place 5 fingers in a single layer in each drawer.
4. Select Zone 1, select BAKE, set temperature to 180°C, and set time to 14 minutes. Select MATCH COOK to match Zone 2 settings to Zone 1. Select START/PAUSE to begin cooking.
5. When cooking is complete, dish out and serve warm.

Cayenne Sesame Nut Mix

SERVES: 4

PREP TIME: 10 minutes
COOK TIME: 5 minutes

15 g buttery spread, melted
10 ml honey
¼ tsp. cayenne pepper
6 g sesame seeds
¼ tsp. coarse salt
¼ tsp. freshly ground black pepper
150 g cashews
150 g almonds
80 g mini pretzels
30 g rice squares cereal
Cooking spray

1. In a large bowl, combine the buttery spread, honey, cayenne pepper, sesame seeds, coarse salt, and black pepper, then add the cashews, almonds, pretzels, and rice squares, tossing to coat.
2. Install a crisper plate in Zone 1 drawer and spray with cooking spray. Arrange the mixture in the drawer, then insert drawer in unit.
3. Select Zone 1, select ROAST, set temperature to 180°C, and set time to 5 minutes. Press the START/PAUSE button to begin cooking.
4. When cooking is complete, remove drawer from unit. Allow to cool for 5 minutes before serving.

Root Veggie Chips with Herb Salt

SERVES: 2

PREP TIME: 10 minutes
COOK TIME: 16 minutes

1 parsnip, washed
1 small beetroot, washed
1 small turnip, washed
½ small sweet potato, washed
5 ml olive oil

Cooking spray
Herb Salt:
¼ tsp. coarse salt
2 tsps. finely chopped fresh parsley

1. Peel and thinly slice the parsnip, beetroot, turnip, and sweet potato, then place the vegetables in a large bowl, add the olive oil, and toss.
2. Insert a crisper plate in both drawer and spray with cooking spray. Place half of the vegetables in a single layer in each drawer.
3. Select Zone 1, select AIR FRY, set temperature to 200°C, and set time to 16 minutes. Select MATCH COOK to match Zone 2 settings to Zone 1. Select START/PAUSE to begin cooking.
4. When the Zone 1 and 2 times reach 8 minutes, press START/PAUSE to pause the unit. Remove the drawers from unit and shake for 10 seconds. Reinsert drawers in unit and press START/PAUSE to resume cooking.
5. While the chips cook, make the herb salt in a small bowl by combining the coarse salt and parsley.
6. When cooking is complete, transfer chips to a serving plate, then sprinkle the herb salt on top and allow to cool for 2 to 3 minutes before serving.

Spiced Sweet Potato Chips

SERVES: 2

PREP TIME: 10 minutes
COOK TIME: 15 minutes

30 ml olive oil
1½ tsps. smoked paprika
1½ tsps. coarse salt, plus more as needed
1 tsp. chilli powder
½ tsp. ground cumin
½ tsp. ground turmeric
½ tsp. mustard powder
¼ tsp. cayenne pepper
2 medium sweet potatoes (about 280 g each), cut into wedges, 1-cm thick and 7-cm long
Freshly ground black pepper, to taste
160 ml sour cream
1 garlic clove, grated

1. In a large bowl, combine the olive oil, paprika, salt, chilli powder, cumin, turmeric, mustard powder, and cayenne. Add the sweet potatoes, season with black pepper, and toss to evenly coat.
2. Install a crisper plate in Zone 1 drawer. Place sweet potatoes in the drawer (save the bowl with the leftover oil and spices), then insert drawer in unit.
3. Select Zone 1, select AIR FRY, set temperature to 200°C, and set time to 15 minutes. Press the START/PAUSE button to begin cooking.
4. With 7 minutes remaining, press START/PAUSE to pause the unit. Remove the drawer from unit and shake for 10 seconds. Reinsert drawer in unit and press START/PAUSE to resume cooking.
5. Return the potato wedges to the reserved bowl and toss again while they are hot.
6. Meanwhile, in a small bowl, stir together the sour cream and garlic. Season with salt and black pepper and transfer to a serving dish.
7. Serve the potato wedges hot with the garlic sour cream.

Peach Parcel

SERVES: 2

PREP TIME: 10 minutes
COOK TIME: 15 minutes

1 peach, peeled, cored and halved
240 ml prepared vanilla custard
2 puff pastry sheets
1 egg, beaten lightly
15 g sugar
Pinch of ground cinnamon
15 ml whipped cream

1. Place a spoonful of vanilla custard and a peach half in the centre of each pastry sheet.
2. Mix sugar and cinnamon in a bowl and sprinkle on the peach halves.
3. Pinch the corners of sheets together to shape into a parcel.
4. Install a crisper plate in Zone 1 drawer. Place parcels in the drawer, then insert drawer in unit.
5. Select Zone 1, select BAKE, set temperature to 170°C, and set time to 15 minutes. Press the START/PAUSE button to begin cooking.
6. When cooking is complete, remove drawer from unit. Top with whipped cream.
7. Dish out and serve with remaining custard.

Healthy Fruit Muffins

SERVES: 6

PREP TIME: 10 minutes
COOK TIME: 10 minutes

240 ml semi-skimmed milk
1 pack Oreo biscuits, crushed
4 g baking soda
4 g baking powder
1 banana, peeled and chopped
1 apple, peeled, cored and chopped
2 g cocoa powder
5 ml honey
5 ml fresh lemon juice
Pinch of ground cinnamon

1. Grease 6 muffin cups lightly.
2. Mix milk, biscuits, cocoa powder, baking soda and baking powder in a bowl until a smooth mixture is formed.
3. Divide this mixture into the prepared muffin cups.
4. Insert a crisper plate in both drawers. Place half of the muffin cups in a single layer in each drawer.
5. Select Zone 1, select BAKE, set temperature to 160°C, and set time to 10 minutes. Select MATCH COOK to match Zone 2 settings to Zone 1. Select START/PAUSE to begin cooking.
6. When cooking is complete, transfer muffin cups to a plate.
7. Mix banana, apple, honey, lemon juice and cinnamon in a bowl.
8. Scoop out some portion from centre of muffins and fill with the fruit mixture.
9. Refrigerate for 2 hours and serve chilled.

Bread Pudding

SERVES: 2

PREP TIME: 10 minutes
COOK TIME: 12 minutes

240 ml milk
1 egg
30 g sultanas, soaked in hot water for about 15 minutes
2 bread slices, cut into small cubes
15 g chocolate chips
12 g brown sugar
½ tsp. ground cinnamon
¼ tsp. vanilla extract
15 g sugar

1. Grease a 18x13 cm baking dish lightly.
2. Mix milk, egg, brown sugar, cinnamon and vanilla extract until well combined.
3. Stir in the sultanas and mix well.
4. Arrange the bread cubes evenly in the baking dish and top with the milk mixture.
5. Refrigerate for about 20 minutes and sprinkle with chocolate chips and sugar.
6. Install a crisper plate in Zone 1 drawer. Place the baking dish in the drawer, then insert drawer in unit.
7. Select Zone 1, select BAKE, set temperature to 190°C, and set time to 12 minutes. Press the START/PAUSE button to begin cooking.
8. When cooking is complete, remove drawer from unit. Transfer bread pudding to a plate. Serve warm.

Pear and Apple Crumble

SERVES: 6

PREP TIME: 10 minutes
COOK TIME: 20 minutes

225 g apples, cored and chopped
225 g pears, cored and chopped
120 g flour
200 g sugar
15 g butter
1 tsp. ground cinnamon
¼ tsp. ground cloves
1 tsp. vanilla extract
30 g chopped walnuts
Whipped cream, for serving

1. Lightly grease a 18x13 cm baking dish and place the apples and pears inside.
2. Combine the rest of the ingredients, minus the walnuts and the whipped cream, until a coarse, crumbly texture is achieved.
3. Pour the mixture over the fruits and spread it evenly. Top with the chopped walnuts.
4. Install a crisper plate in Zone 1 drawer. Place the baking dish in the drawer, then insert drawer in unit.
5. Select Zone 1, select BAKE, set temperature to 170°C, and set time to 20 minutes. Press the START/PAUSE button to begin cooking, until the top turns golden brown.
6. Serve at room temperature with whipped cream.

Buttered Bread Rolls

SERVES: 12

PREP TIME: 15 minutes
COOK TIME: 23 minutes

cooking spray
240 ml milk
360 g plain flour
105 g unsalted butter
15 ml coconut oil
15 ml olive oil
1 tsp. yeast
Salt and black pepper, to taste

1. Put olive oil, milk and coconut oil in a pan and cook for about 3 minutes.
2. Remove from the heat and mix well.
3. Mix together plain flour, yeast, butter, salt and black pepper in a large bowl.
4. Knead well for about 5 minutes until a dough is formed.
5. Cover the dough with a damp cloth and keep aside for about 5 minutes in a warm place.
6. Knead the dough for about 5 minutes again with your hands.
7. Cover the dough with a damp cloth and keep aside for about 30 minutes in a warm place.
8. Divide the dough into 12 equal pieces and roll each into a ball.
9. Insert a crisper plate in both drawer and spray with cooking spray. Place 6 balls in a single layer in each drawer.
10. Select Zone 1, select BAKE, set temperature to 180°C, and set time to 20 minutes. Select MATCH COOK to match Zone 2 settings to Zone 1. Select START/PAUSE to begin cooking.
11. When cooking is complete, transfer balls to a plate. Serve warm.

APPENDIX 1:
NINJA DUAL ZONE AIR FRY TIMETABLE

Air Fry Cooking Chart

INGREDIENT	AMOUNT	PREPARATION	TOSS IN OIL	TEMP	COOK TIME
VEGETABLES					
Asparagus	200g	Whole, stems trimmed	2 tsp	200°C	8-12 mins
Beetroot	6 small or 4 large (about 1kg)	Whole	None	200°C	35-45 mins
Bell peppers (for roasting)	2 peppers	Whole	None	200°C	16 mins
Broccoli	1 head (400g)	Cut in 2.5cm florets	1 Tbsp	200°C	9 mins
Brussel sprouts	500g	Cut in half, stem removed	1 Tbsp	200°C	15-20 mins
Butternut squash	500g-750g	Cut in 2.5cm pieces	1 Tbsp	200°C	20-25 mins
Carrots	500g	Peeled, cut in 1.5cm pieces	1 Tbsp	200°C	13-16 mins
Cauliflower	1 head (900g)	Cut in 2.5cm florets	2 Tbsp	200°C	15-20 mins
Corn on the cob	4 ears	Whole ears, husks removed	1 Tbsp	200°C	12-15 mins
Courgette	500g	Cut in quarters lengthwise, then cut in 2.5cm pieces	1 Tbsp	200°C	15-18 mins
Fine green beans	200g	Trimmed	1 Tbsp	200°C	8 mins
Kale (for crisps)	100g	Torn in pieces, stems removed	None	150°C	8 mins
Mushrooms	225g	Wiped, cut in quarters	1 Tbsp	200°C	7 mins
Potatoes, white e.g. King Edward, Maris Piper or Russet	750g	Cut in 2.5cm wedges	1 Tbsp	200°C	18-20 mins
	450g	Hand-cut chips, thin	½-3 Tbsp, vegetable oil	200°C	20-24 mins
	450g	Hand-cut chips, thick	½-3 Tbsp, vegetable oil	200°C	23-26 mins
	4 whole (200g each)	Pierced with fork 3 times	None	200°C	25 mins
Potatoes, sweet	750g	Cut in 2.5cm chunks	1 Tbsp	200°C	15-20 mins
	4 whole (225g each)	Pierced with fork 3 times	None	200°C	30-35 mins
POULTRY					
Chicken breasts	2 breasts (200g each)	None	Brushed with oil	190°C	22-25 mins
	4 breasts (150-175g each)	None	Brushed with oil	190°C	34 mins
Chicken thighs	4 thighs (200g each)	Bone in	Brushed with oil	200°C	22-28 mins
	4 thighs (100g each)	Boneless	Brushed with oil	200°C	18-22 mins
Chicken wings	1kg	Drumettes & flats	1 Tbsp	200°C	33 mins
FISH & SEAFOOD					
Fish cakes	2 cakes (145g each)	None	Brushed with oil	200°C	15 mins
Salmon fillets	2 fillets	None	Brushed with oil	200°C	10-13 mins
Prawns	16 large	Whole, peeled, tails on	1 Tbsp	200°C	7-10 mins

Air Fry Cooking Chart

INGREDIENT	AMOUNT	PREPARATION	TOSS IN OIL	TEMP	COOK TIME
BEEF					
Burgers	4 quarter-pounders	2.5cm thick	None	190°C	12 mins
Steaks	2 steaks (230g each)	Whole	None	200°C	22 mins
PORK					
Bacon	4 strips, cut in half	None	None	180°C	9 mins
Pork chops	2 thick-cut, bone-in chops	Bone in	Brushed with oil	190°C	19 mins
	4 boneless chops	Boneless	Brushed with oil	190°C	18 mins
Pork loin steaks	2 steaks (400g)	Whole	Brushed with oil	180°C	17 mins
Sausages	4 sausages	Whole	None	200°C	16 mins
Gammon steaks	1 steak (225g)	Cut rind at 2cm, turn over after 5 mins	Brushed with oil	180°C	10 mins
LAMB					
Lamb chops	4 chops (340g)	None	Brushed with oil	200°C	12 mins
Lamb steaks	3 steaks (300g)	None	Brushed with oil	200°C	12 mins
FROZEN FOODS					
Chicken nuggets	1 box (397g)	None	None	200°C	16 mins
Breaded fish fillets	4 fillets (Total 500g)	None	None	200°C	14-16 mins
Fish fingers	10	None	None	200°C	15 mins
French fries	500g	None	None	180°C	20 mins
French fries	1kg	None	None	180°C	42 mins
Sweet potato chips	450g	None	None	190°C	20 mins
Hash browns	7	Single layer	None	200°C	15 mins
Fish fillets in batter	4	Turn halfway	None	180°C	18 mins
Scampi in breadcrumbs	280g	None	None	180°C	12 mins
Prawn tempura	8 prawns (total 140g)	Turn halfway	None	190°C	8-9 mins
Chunky oven chips	500g	None	None	180°C	20 mins
Potato wedges	500g	None	None	180°C	20 mins
Roast potatoes	700g	None	None	190°C	20 mins
Vegan burgers	4	Single layer	None	180°C	10 mins
Battered onion rings	300g	None	None	190°C	14 mins
Breaded garlic mushrooms	300g	None	None	190°C	10-12 mins
Chicken goujons	11	None	None	190°C	8 mins
Chicken Kiev	4	None	None	180°C	15 mins
Yorkshire pudding	8 (total 150g)	None	None	180°C	3-4 mins

Max Crisp Cooking Chart

INGREDIENT	AMOUNT	PREPARATION	TEMP	DEHYDRATE TIME
FROZEN FOOD				
Chicken nuggets	350g (24 nuggets)	None	None	10 mins
Chicken wings	1kg	None	1 Tbsp	17 mins
Popcorn chicken	850g	None	None	6-8 mins
Sweet potato fries	500g	None	1 Tbsp	17 mins
French fries	500g	None	None	8 mins
French fries	1kg	None	None	25 mins
Onion rings	300g	None	None	9 mins

Dehydrate Chart

INGREDIENTS	PREPARATION	TEMP	DEHYDRATE TIME
FRUITS & VEGETABLES			
Apples	Core removed, cut in 3mm slices, rinsed in lemon water, patted dry	60°C	7-8 hours
Asparagus	Cut in 2.5cm pieces, blanched	60°C	6-8 hours
Bananas	Peeled, cut in 3mm slices	60°C	8-10 hours
Beetroot	Peeled, cut in 3mm slices	60°C	6-8 hours
Aubergine	Peeled, cut in 3mm slices, blanched	60°C	6-8 hours
Fresh herbs	Rinsed, patted dry, stems removed	60°C	4 hours
Ginger root	Cut in 3mm slices	60°C	6 hours
Mangoes	Peeled, cut in 3mm slices, pit removed	60°C	6-8 hours
Mushrooms	Cleaned with soft brush (do not wash)	60°C	6-8 hours
Pineapple	Peeled, cored, cut in 3mm-1.25cm slices	60°C	6-8 hours
Strawberries	Cut in half or in 1.25cm slices	60°C	6-8 hours
Tomatoes	Cut in 3mm slices or grated; steam if planning to rehydrate	60°C	6-8 hours
MEAT, POULTRY, FISH			
Beef jerky	Cut in 6mm slices, marinated overnight	70°C	5-7 hours
Chicken jerky	Cut in 6mm slices, marinated overnight	70°C	5-7 hours
Salmon jerky	Cut in 6mm slices, marinated overnight	70°C	3-5 hours
Turkey jerky	Cut in 6mm slices, marinated overnight	70°C	5-7 hours

NOTE There is no temperature adjustment available or necessary when using the Max Crisp function.

Using DualZone Technology: SYNC

RECIPE	AMOUNT	MIX THESE INGREDIENTS	FUNCTION	TEMP/TIME
Fish Cakes	2 fish cakes	Brush with melted butter	Air Fry	200°C | 15 minutes
Balsamic Roasted Tomatoes	500g cherry tomatoes	60ml balsamic vinegar, 1 Tbsp vegetable oil	Roast	200°C | 15 minutes
Honey Sage Pork Chops	2-3 boneless pork chops (120g each)	1 Tbsp vegetable oil, 1 Tbsp honey	Roast	200°C | 17-20 minutes
Cajun Russet Potatoes	4 medium potatoes, diced	2 Tbsp vegetable oil, 2 Tbsp Cajun seasoning	Air Fry	200°C | 30 minutes
Green Beans with Almonds	500g green beans, ends trimmed	2 Tbsp vegetable oil, 60g sliced almonds	Air Fry	200°C | 8-10 minutes
Miso Glazed Salmon	3 salmon fillets (170g each)	2 Tbsp miso paste, 1 Tsp vegetable oil, rub onto salmon	Air Fry	200°C | 15 minutes
Honey Hazelnut Brussel Sprouts	500g Brussel sprouts, cut in half	2 Tbsp vegetable oil, 60ml honey, 60g chopped hazelnuts	Air Fry	200°C | 23 minutes
Buffalo Chicken Thighs	4 boneless skin-on chicken thighs (110-140g each)	240ml buffalo sauce, toss with chicken	Air Fry	200°C | 27 minute
Plant Based "Meat" Burger	500g plant-based ground "meat" (4 125g burgers)	1 Tbsp minced garlic, 1 Tbsp minced onion	Air Fry	190°C | 20 minute
Mediterranean Cauliflower	1 head cauliflower, cut in 1.5cm florets	120ml tahini, 2 Tbsp vegetable oil	Air Fry	200°C | 35 minutes
French Fries	500g French fries	Season as desired	Air Fry	200°C | 20 minutes
Corn on the cob	4 Cobettes	Brush with melted butter	Roast	180°C | 15 minutes

APPENDIX 2: RECIPES INDEX

Printed in Great Britain
by Amazon

53865127R00044